To Art Carey —

You were the key
component to
making this happen!

Great job.
forever grateful,

Dave Luther

DAVE LIEBER

BAD DAD

ALSO BY DAVE LIEBER

Shop at www.YankeeCowboy.com/store

Dave Lieber's
Watchdog Nation:
Bite Back When
Businesses and Scammers
Do You Wrong

(also available as e-book and CD audio book)

The Dog of My Nightmares:
Stories by Texas Columnist
Dave Lieber

(also available as CD audio book)

The High-Impact Writer:
Ideas, Tips & Strategies to Turn
Your Writing World Upside Down

I Knew Rufe Snow Before He Was a Road

(with Tim Bedison)

Give Us a Big Hug

(with Tim Bedison)

DAVE LIEBER

BAD DAD

Special thanks to the
Fort Worth Star-Telegram

YANKEE
COWBOY
PUBLISHING

P.O. Box 123
Keller, TX 76244-0123
1-800-557-8166
www.YankeeCowboy.com
publisher@yankeecowboy.com

For Austin James Lieber

Son, you are an amazing boy. I'm proud of you.
Thanks for giving me permission to share our story.

All my love forever,
Dad

I shall be telling this with a sigh
Somewhere ages and ages hence:
Two roads diverged in a wood, and I —
I took the one less traveled by,
And that has made all the difference.

— Robert Frost
The Road Not Taken (1916)

She took the baby on her arm, and, with a burning blush, and yet a haughty smile, and a glance that would not be abashed, looked around at her townspeople and neighbours. On the breast of her gown, in fine red cloth, surrounded with an elaborate embroidery and fantastic flourishes of gold thread, appeared the letter A.

— Nathaniel Hawthorne
The Scarlet Letter (1850)

The following is a true story.

I first got stopped by an officer from the small-town police department about a month after moving to Texas. My new neighbors in Fort Worth had warned me about a strip of roadway across the street in the neighboring city of Watauga. That strip contained Watauga's police headquarters, City Hall, the biggest Baptist church in town and a drive-through McDonald's. A speed trap, they said. I remembered that fact a little too late after I forgot to brake coming down a hill and saw flashing police lights in my rearview mirror. When asked, I told the officer I was new in town, learning my way. He let me go with a warning.

The second time I got summoned by the city came a few weeks later when the town's "honorary police chief" demanded that I come see him in his office. He was the Watauga city manager and former police chief, and the honorary title allowed him to keep his gun. I knew why he wanted me.

In my new job as a metro columnist for the

Fort Worth Star-Telegram, I had written my first column about Watauga City Hall. Maybe he liked it. I drove less than a mile from my new house to his City Hall office situated on that strip. Inside, dark-eyed Bill Keating ordered me to sit, then slammed a copy of my newspaper on his desk.

"Don't you dare write another word about Watauga, Texas, without talking with me first! You got that, son?"

"Yes, I do."

"I'm serious, son."

"Yes, sir."

The third time I got stopped, a police officer pulled me over and asked to see my driver's license. When he saw my name, he surprised me by introducing himself and shaking my hand. He thanked me for supporting him in a battle with his superiors. Lucky me. I had written a column arguing that after a gallant act he had performed sheltering a young abused girl, he was treated unfairly and punished. After the public learned of his story, they rallied behind him. Before this traffic stop, he and I had never met. We talked by the side of the road. Again—no ticket.

The fourth time came several years later, after writing many more columns about the town's police and fire departments and city government. By then, I was known among the officers for my writings. Some liked me; others didn't. Once again, though, I got lucky. The officer who stopped me for speeding let me go with a warning. Later, though, he was scolded by the chief, who heard about it on the police radio. The officer told me later that his chief chewed him out because he wanted to make sure the officer understood the department's informal rule:

"You never let Dave Lieber go with only a warning."

Then there was that fifth time. The stop that has made all the difference.

Here's what I remember:

Aug. 13, 2008

My son Austin, 11, and I are eating breakfast inside that McDonald's on the strip. He's my boy, my pride, so much like me. Attentive. Creative. A fast car in the fast lane. I try to get Austin to slow down, but he moves faster than anyone I know. On the basketball court or running down the stairs at home. He can't stand waiting. He has to keep moving.

On this day, though, things don't go well for either of us. Austin finishes his pancakes. He wants to go. I'm not done. I start sipping a hot coffee and read the newspaper. This drives him batty. He wants to go home and call a friend so they can play.

"Sit and wait until I'm done, please! I want to finish my coffee."

"Let's go, Dad! I want to go now!"

"I'm telling you: sit and wait until I'm done."

"No, let's go." He says it louder. "I want to leave now!"

"Shut up! We're in a restaurant. Go sit and wait

for me at that table. If you don't, I'm going to let you walk home. You can think about the way you behaved during your walk."

Several men are sitting at nearby tables by themselves. All have their backs to us. But we are loud enough that they can hear.

Next thing I know, I'm fast-walking out the door. Austin is right behind me. I speed up. He speeds up. Outside in the parking lot, I unlock the car, jump in and then lock the doors before he can get in.

I turn on the engine and back the car out. He's still pulling on the handle. When he sees the car moving backward, he lets go but chases me for several steps. Then he stops.

He's standing in the parking lot, crying and bewildered.

I drive away.

Later I learned that several adults gathered around him. One asked Austin if they should call the police. Austin, then 5-foot-3 and capable of walking the 7/10th of a mile, or six blocks, through our neighborhood back to our house, shrugged his shoulders. He wasn't sure what to do.

I drive up the road to cool down. I call my wife, Karen, at work and tell her what happened. She tells me to turn around and get him. I make a U-turn.

Ten minutes or more have passed. If he's not at McDonald's, I'll cruise the route he would take and make sure he's headed home. But in front of

McDonald's, as I pull in, I see a small crowd. Several men turn and glare at me.

I see two Watauga police cars. The officers are waiting for me.

So that's the fifth time I got stopped by Watauga authorities. The one that in the days ahead would make it possible for me to lose so much: my son, my career of 30 years, my job, my good name.

Take your worst 10 minutes of any day. You acted terribly, but maybe nobody knew. Or at least you thought so. Then imagine that everyone finds out. Everyone.

Within days, your foolishness flashes around the world. What you did is featured on the TV news, in newspapers, on radio talk shows and overheated cable-television debates, and in blogs. Everybody has an opinion about you and what you did in those 10 minutes.

Everybody decides whether you are a good dad or a bad dad.

One of the officers greets me by name.

"You're Dave Lieber, right?"

He asks to see my driver's license. He tells me that terrible things could have happened to my son while I was gone. He tells me to stand by myself and wait by the front of McDonald's.

I stand there, like a rock. Eventually, an officer introduces himself by name, but he says it so fast I can't make it out.

"Here's what's going to happen. We're going

to do a report for today's occurrence, OK? We've gathered witness statements from all the witnesses here. We are not going to take any action today with you, which we could. We are going to refer this case to Child Protective Services. We are going to turn it over to our investigation division, and they will give a referral to the district attorney's office. I don't know what the outcome of that will be. That's beyond my area.

"But I just wanted you to be aware of the severity of the circumstances today—I'm sure you probably already are aware of that—and the actions that could take place. We are not going to do that, though, today. And we will leave it up to the process down the road to see what happens. But just keep in mind and be aware that there could be a later date that you will have to answer to a higher cause than us, OK?"

"Yes, sir."

"So keep that in mind. Is there going to be a problem between you and your son now?"

"No."

Another officer approaches.

"Obviously, having had to stand here and think of it, you understand everything that could go wrong, and what our responsibilities are as parents?"

"I do. Thank you."

He says we can go home.

We are in the car, driving home.

"Sorry, Daddy."

Those are the first words out of Austin's mouth. I am relieved to hear them.

"Well, there could be some serious stuff coming out of this," I say. "This will go everywhere."

He tells me that after I left him and the men gathered around, he said he told them: "It was my fault. I was just being mean."

One of the men responded, "No, it doesn't matter what you did. Your dad should never drive off like that."

He also tells me that when the officers found out who his father is, they called in "a higher officer."

Driving us home, I look down and see I'm still holding the cup of coffee I bought at the restaurant. The coffee is cold now.

That's what I remember.

At home.

First, I tend to my son. We talk about what happened. He asks me to apologize, too. Sounds like a good idea. I don't hesitate. We talk about his behavior. We talk about mine, too.

Karen rushes home from work. We are surprised to see her. She quickly scolds: "I don't know what the heck you two were thinking."

The incident is about an hour old when I call my longtime editor, Lois Norder, the managing editor for news and investigations.

"Hey, this is in the category of you better hear it from me first."

The boss listens. Then she says she must hang up and tell the executive editor. A few hours later, Norder calls back and suggests that I write a column about what happened and what I have learned. She tells me to call parenting experts and find out what to do in that kind of situation.

It isn't an outlandish request. Two times a week,

I write "The Watchdog" column. I expose wrongdoing by businesses, governments and others. I write about people's mistakes, and how to fix them. Sometimes, I write about my own mistakes.

A column would be the way to get the story out on my terms. No matter what happens, people can understand that I didn't mean to be a bad dad. Most important, they'd see that I have learned something. And maybe the column will help others. That's what I do for a living.

Writing about my family is not out of the ordinary. Actually, for me, it's the norm. Before I became The Watchdog, I wrote a metro column that alternated hard-hitting investigative stories about the goings-on in 21 cities and six school districts with soft tear-jerker family stories. I thought if readers knew my family and saw similarities with their own lives, they'd be more inclined to pay attention when I turned serious in my writings. And for a dozen years, at least until this moment, it had worked.

I had even proposed marriage to Karen and her two children, Jonathan, 10, and Desiree, 12, in the newspaper in 1994. ("Here in Texas, I've met the woman of my dreams. Unfortunately, she lives with the dog of my nightmares," it began.) The marriage proposal column won first

The woman of my dreams, Karen (left), and her children, Desiree and Jonathan, after I proposed in my newspaper column.

place in the 1995 National Society of Newspaper Columnists contest. I had a new wife with two adorable children that I loved as my own. I had plenty to write about.

Austin's arrival in 1997 was, aside from my wedding, the most joyous day of my life. I couldn't wait to write about him. I didn't even wait for his birth. I announced I'd be a dad by writing an open letter to the as-yet-unborn baby. It ran as my Sunday column.

My darling little Beaver Cleaver Lieber,

I haven't told the world about you yet because your pending arrival is just starting to sink in. Your existence hit me full force last week when your mother and I visited the obstetrician's office. We looked at a sonogram screen showing an image of you inside of her. My goodness, you look about the size of my finger.

"That's the fetus," the doctor said. "See the little flicker?"

I saw your little heart thumping away. I saw your little head and arms, your emerging eye sockets and tiny nose. Kid, you are the most incredible thing I have ever seen.

Since we don't have a name for you, I'm going with the working title of Beaver Cleaver Lieber after one of my favorite television characters. Beaver's father, Ward, always took a genuine interest in his son's activities and escapades. And that's the way I view fatherhood, too.

Last week, in your honor, I placed an old photograph of Ward and little Beaver on our fireplace mantle. In the photograph, Ward looks sternly at Beaver because, inevitably, the Beav has stumbled into trouble again.

Little one, I was always hesitant to have a child of my own because of my late mother's great prophesy. As a child, whenever I misbehaved, my mother warned, "God is going to punish you when you have children."

Now I have two stepchildren, and they are so wonderful and even-tempered that, obviously, they do not share my genetic material.

But you, little Beav, you have the power to make my mother's words come true. So this is my first official request as your daddy. Please be calm. My mother didn't have to be right about everything.

Your half sister, Desiree, and half brother, Jonathan, eagerly await your arrival next spring. But we won't ever use that "half" word again, because there will be nothing halfway about their love for you.

Your sister is a 14-year-old high school freshman. She's very tall and wants to be a model. Further proof that she does not carry my genetic material.

Your brother is a 12-year-old Little League allstar. He definitely expects you to pitch by the 1998 season.

Both are trying to come up with your name: Jonathan likes Scooter; Desiree favors Alessandra.

"It can't be a run-of-the-mill name," your mother says.

Until we decide, I'll call you Beav.

Speaking of your mother, you're quite lucky to have her. Karen is a nurturing and kind-hearted woman. But you know that, don't you?

Your grandparents—Karen's parents—can't wait to meet you. And your other grandfather— my father—cried when he first heard about you, probably because I told him on my late mother's birthday.

Finally, in our household, there is Dr. Nero, the elderly black cat with an honorary degree in philosophy, and Sadie the Psycho Dog, whose story is too complicated for now. They will love you and care for you, too.

Nobody, though, awaits you more than I. Desiree and Jonathan are the wonders of my life, but I can't take credit for their success. Since I only married into the family 20 months ago, I missed their important early years.

What kind of father will I be from scratch?

I can't wait to see your first breath, your first steps, your first day at school. Can't wait to push your little bicycle with the training wheels. Can't wait for the day when the wheels come off, and I let you go.

I want to get us, I mean you, an old-fashioned red wagon and pull you around the neighborhood. Since you will be the first native Texan in our family, we can go in search of the Alamo.

Little Beav, there's so much more to say. Just know that I cannot wait to meet you, hug you, kiss you. Welcome to our family.

This was an emotional announcement, unusual for a newspaper column. Readers liked it well enough that I returned with Act 2, his birth announcement. Austin James Lieber, born May 2, 1997, may have been the first baby in recorded history to document his trip through the birth canal in a daily newspaper column.

The day he came home from the hospital, a *Star-Telegram* photographer appeared at our house and took a photograph of him while he rested in his new crib. That photograph was used as his column photo. His debut column appeared two days after his birth, on May 4, 1997.

> *Howdy, everybody.*
>
> *I'm Austin James Lieber, one of Northeast Tarrant County's newest residents. Yes, I'm finally here. At last we get to meet.*
>
> *On Friday, I gave Mommy the greatest gift I could. I arrived on her 41st birthday. The clock read 1:02 p.m.*
>
> *"Welcome to the world, kid!" Daddy said.*
>
> *My journey out here hurt. It was real scary. But I was getting too crowded inside. Native Texan that I am, I wanted more real estate.*
>
> *Slowly at first, Mommy pushed and squeezed me toward my new life. I was quite unsure what awaited me. But I was eager to meet my family and new friends.*
>
> *Mommy asked me to work with her, so I tried my best.*
>
> *"You're a good boy," she kept saying during our*

shared four-hour struggle. "A very good boy."

Once I heard her scream, "Ooooh!!! I hate the pain. I know he does, too. Come on, Austin! Hurry up! Come out!"

So I did. Already, I'm starting to forget the pain.

Hello, world. I'm happy to be here.

I weigh 7 pounds 2 ounces and am 19 inches long. I have blue eyes and dark curly hair. I have Daddy's grin, but not necessarily his personality, because I hardly ever complain.

It's wonderful to match my family's voices with their faces. Moments after I arrived, my delivery-man, Dr. Robert Hardie, placed me on Mommy's tummy. I lay staring at her and smiling. She's prettier than I ever dreamed.

My big sister is really cool. Desiree held me tight, and I held her back. My big brother was so happy to see me that he cried. At first, I thought he wanted milk, but Daddy explained that Jonathan cries for joy at momentous occasions.

Daddy, Jonathan and I have already formed a secret boys club called the Lieber-teers. Daddy is

president, Jonathan is vice president, and I'm secretary-treasurer. What's a secretary-treasurer?

Daddy read somewhere that babies are most aware of their surroundings during their first two hours of life. So he crammed my brain full of necessary information.

He told me where I live and about my name. Austin is the capital of Texas, he said, and I'm the first native Texan in the family. He told me to be proud.

Daddy also sat with me in a rocking chair and read aloud the Ten Commandments. He said I needed a proper start in life. But when he read the one about honoring thy mother and father, I looked up and wanted to say, "Duh, Dad."

"Wonderful introduction to the world," said my nurse, Eulee Phillips of Bedford. Yeah, maybe so, but I had to admit that I have a higher priority.

I turned to Mommy and cried out, "Got milk?"

I have a silver rattle that makes a funny noise. It's the same rattle Daddy played with almost 40 years ago. I'm surprised it still works.

But life is about more than playing. There's work to do. Daddy made me write this column for you.

"What should I write about?" I asked.

"Write about your life and times," he suggested.

"What life and times?" I asked. "I'm only a day old. I haven't done anything yet."

That doesn't stop other newspaper columnists, he said.

Well, there's something I can say that Daddy never can.

I'm a native Texan.

I understand what that means. It's an honor. And I promise to do my very best to make y'all proud.

Oh, one more thing.

Got milk?

So it wasn't unusual to mix my stories between home and hearth and school board and police department. This variety kept readers guessing. Kept me enthusiastic about my job, too. Nobody, not even me, knew what to expect in a Dave Lieber column.

One thing they could expect, though, was a sharp focus on wrongdoing. I grew up during the Watergate era. Saw Woodward and Bernstein speak a half-dozen times. Knew by heart details of their adventures investigating the Nixon White House. As part of my columnist training, I studied ethics, government, politics and writing. I had the heart of a public servant, wanting to do good for the world.

Getting to the point where I could perform that task in my new home—Fort Worth, Texas—without getting pilloried was my toughest challenge. I was an outsider who had never been to Texas before. Yet I was expected to write about Texas as if I knew something, anything. Before I could write about Texas, though, I had to get right with Texas, and that was no small thing.

In 1993, Michael Blackman, the editor of the *Fort Worth Star-Telegram*, recruited me from the *Philadelphia Inquirer*, where I had worked 10 years as a reporter. He invited me to write a metro column for Fort Worth's northern suburbs. He said, "I want to bring New York-style journalism to Texas."

Basically, what he meant was he was feeding me to the wolves.

When I arrived in Texas in the summer of 1993 (don't move to Texas in the summer of *any* year), I was clearly the wrong guy in the wrong place. My audience consisted mostly of native Texans who were married, Baptist, Republican and conservative. These good folks didn't ask the *Star-Telegram* to send a new columnist who was a liberal, divorced, Democratic, New York City Jew.

What a struggle to connect with Texans. They'd ask me questions for which I always had the wrong answer:

Texan: Boy, whar you from?

Me: New York City.

Texan: New York City? Git a rope!

But Texans are among the friendliest folks. They didn't give up on me.

Texan: What church do you go to?

Me: I don't go to church.

Texan: Why not? Don't you believe in the Lord?

Me: No, I do believe in the Lord.

Texan: Then why don't you go to church?

Me: 'Cause I'm Jewish.

Some Texans would stutter and step back. A few would name Jewish people they knew and ask if I knew them.

"No. It's a big tribe."

Sometimes I was told that I was going to hell because I hadn't accepted Jesus Christ as my Lord and Savior.

Welcome to Texas, boy.

My beginning was hardly smooth. The first week I wrote a column that I wished afterward I could take back.

> *I'm going to have my first chicken-fried steak.*
>
> *I never heard of it before I arrived in Texas, and I can't understand its unchallenged popularity. Just a piece of fried meat, right?... As soon as I hit Texas, though, I started hearing talk about the chicken-fried steak. It was more brag than talk. ...*
>
> *I must cut through the mystique of the chicken-fried steak. And I must learn the answer to a riddle that keeps me awake at nights:*
>
> *IS IT CHICKEN OR IS IT STEAK?*

Quite a stupid way to begin a relationship with my new audience. But there's no training manual showing one how to move to a new state, start a newspaper column and immediately win the hearts and minds of his audience. Heck, I didn't know what made Texans laugh or cry. I didn't understand their language, their customs, music, food, penchant for Texas flags and blue jeans (which I mistakenly called "cowboy dungarees" the first time I went into a Western-wear store).

The one thing I could do, though, was investigate and get all sides of a story and share these findings with readers in a compelling narrative. That's why I got the job. And one area best-suited to my skills was my coverage of small police departments.

Decades before, as a student at the University of Pennsylvania in Philadelphia, I cut my teeth on what I consider the biggest story of my life.

1977

I am 19 years old and a sophomore columnist for the student newspaper, *The Daily Pennsylvanian*. My roommate hears something from a friend that he considers astonishing. He rushes home to tell me.

He has learned that the campus police are sending students as undercover spies into meetings of campus political groups. These student spies write summary reports of what they hear and see. They sign their reports with code names like Mickey Mouse and Donald Duck. The campus police then distribute the reports to the Philadelphia police and the FBI.

College students are spying on other students! The spies even get paid as part of their federally funded work-study jobs. I spend eight months researching the story. At first, campus police officials deny it, but I wear them down and, eventually, they tell me why they do it.

After my story appears on Page One, several top officials at Penn are fired. The story makes *The New York Times*, which hires me as its campus stringer. And I win a $500 award from the university administration for "promoting social change." I am hooked on this journalism thing. I know I can do this for a living.

After graduation, I gained experience covering local, county and state government for newspapers in Florida, West Virginia, Georgia and Pennsylvania. I love my work. Being a newspaperman is a cherished honor. You ask questions. Hold people accountable. Save taxpayers money. Make the community a better place. And you have a lot of fun, too.

Imagine, though, for a moment, that as part of your job, you have the power to write tickets to police departments and city governments the way they write tickets and issue fines to you. When they do something that isn't right, you issue a citation seen by hundreds of thousands of newspaper readers. What you find out about them goes on their permanent record. Not in the court of law, but in the court of public opinion. That's what a newspaperman or woman can do.

For a dozen years, whenever I saw any government agency in the many towns and school districts I covered engage in questionable behavior, I wrote them a ticket. I wrote more than 100 columns a year about many topics. Watauga had its share of these tickets with revealing stories about its city government, police and firefighters. Unluckily for them, I live across the street from the city and its speed-trap strip. That makes it easier to keep an eye on things. Plus, there's something about the little town of 23,497 people, especially its government, that brings you back again and again.

CITATION AND COMPLAINT

0001

TICKET #1 — PRANK 911 CALLS

My first Watauga police story. 1994. Late one night, a records clerk for Watauga police decides to play a joke on the dispatcher on duty. After a night of drinking, she makes prank 911 calls from pay phones around town. When a patrol officer sees her out driving, he stops her. She and her car fit the description given by a convenience store employee who saw the person making 911 calls. The records clerk, who is trained as a backup dispatcher, denies any involvement. The officer tells her to go home.

After an internal investigation, the clerk receives a three-day suspension without pay. In my first column about the police department, I call the suspension weak and write that the backup dispatcher ought to be fired.

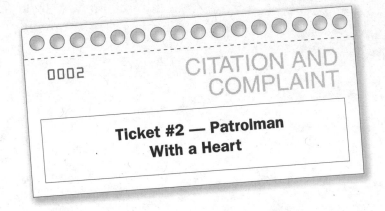

CITATION AND COMPLAINT

0002

Ticket #2 — Patrolman With a Heart

For several days, Officer Roy Woolbright, his wife and four children give temporary shelter to a 13-year-old bruised and battered girl who is a victim of child abuse. Afterward, he is suspended for two days without pay because his superiors say he got personally involved. Others see it as a gallant act.

In the newspaper, I write an open letter to Officer Woolbright:

It must have been a terrible situation at the school. The injured girl was crying, but there was no place to take her—except home to her father, who was later charged with injury to a child.

Child Protective Services officials didn't know what to do. One agency official at the school told you there were no foster homes available.

You talked to your supervisor, Deputy Chief Gary Johnson, and asked him for permission to temporarily house the teen with your family.

Police Chief Bobby Whitmire says Johnson told you not to get involved. But Johnson also told you that whatever you did on your own time was your own business. He sent a mixed signal.

The teen's father gave you verbal permission to shelter his daughter.

You asked the state agency official if your wife should take the girl home, instead of you, but you were told that wasn't necessary.

So you went home and changed out of uniform so you would not be acting in an official capacity when you returned to take the teen home.

Then for five days, your family cared for that child, asking nothing in return. For five days, the Woolbrights went beyond the call of duty.

What an extraordinary example of community service.

No wonder displeased callers have been ringing up Watauga City Hall (817-281-8047) to protest this outrage.

Sir, if you are to be suspended for violating policies against conflict of interest and disobeying an order, then your supervisor ought to take a two-day hike, too. Deputy Chief Johnson failed to give a direct and clear order when his leadership in a most difficult situation was required.

The worst part of this?

You now have a great excuse not to care anymore.

You say, "If I had to do it over again, I wouldn't get as involved."

Many of us feel in our hearts that you were

treated unfairly by your own department.

Right now, there's something we can do to help. Send a little something to help your family overcome your two-day loss of income. Please accept our small gifts of gratitude. It's the least we can do for a hero. (Send it to Roy Woolbright, c/o Watauga Public Safety, 7101 Whitley Road, Watauga, Texas 76148.)

Officer, please remember that your suspension hurts not only you and your family. Your suspension causes many of us pain, too.

It means we are a step closer to a society that teaches its best people not to get involved. Not to care. Not to try to make a difference.

Disciplinary action is supposed to teach a lesson, but this seems like the very worst lesson of all.

0003

CITATION AND COMPLAINT

Ticket #3 — Mute the Citizenry

At a public meeting of the Watauga City Council, I watch the town mayor order his wife, who is speaking at the lectern, to stop talking.

"Sit down."

She keeps talking.

"Sit down! Please!"

Finally, she listens to the mayor, her husband, and sits.

I learn that this city council is one of the few that does not allow citizens to speak to town leaders on a subject of their choosing at a public meeting.

In my column, I quote a councilwoman saying, "Our council meetings are to conduct city business and not have a town meeting. We have lives outside of that chamber. We got out of Monday's meeting at 11 p.m."

I write:

> *Boo hoo.*
>
> *If you live in Watauga, there could come a time when something gets your goat and you want to speak up about it — without official approval. There could be problems in that. Just ask the mayor's wife.*
>
> *If you agree that Watauga should allow an unfettered public comments portion during its meetings, call City Hall at 817-281-8047 and leave a message for your council members.*

People call and complain. New York-style journalism. Starting to take hold.

Within hours of my leaving Austin at McDonald's and my encounter with police, I am writing a column about it. One of thousands I have written. But this one is different. This one is a ticket to myself.

A PARENT LEARNS
FROM A SERIOUS MISTAKE

By Dave Lieber/The Watchdog
Fort Worth Star-Telegram
Aug. 15, 2008

In this job, I talk to people about the difference between right and wrong and how to handle troubling matters.

While I learn about the matters and try to help others, I also learn about myself. I'm a human being and I make mistakes, too.

Some are stupid. Some are serious.

The other day, I made a stupid and quite serious mistake that I want to share with you.

As a parent, I understand—as do most parents—how our children can say and do things that cause us to react in an emotional way. In our household, we call it "pushing buttons." My 11-year-old son pushed mine pretty hard.

We went out to breakfast the other morning at a restaurant. As soon as he had finished eating, he demanded that we leave. But I wasn't done. I asked him to please be patient. He refused. I told him, not asked him, to wait. Same response from him. This went on and on and on.

I sent him to another table. I tried to ignore him. But my buttons were pushed. Finally, I couldn't take it anymore. I stormed out of the restaurant and told him to walk the few blocks home.

I got in the car and drove off.

I was gone for several minutes, long enough to calm down. I doubled back to the restaurant to pick him up. By then, two police cars and a small crowd were gathered outside.

A caring patron had called the police.

My son had given his statement. He explained what he had done. The officer asked if any blows were exchanged. None were.

The police officer gave me a stern lecture about being a responsible parent. He said that it doesn't take more than a few minutes for something to happen to an unsupervised child. He said, "As a journalist, you know this."

My son apologized to me, and I apologized to

him. The officer asked if we were OK to go home. Properly chastened, we were.

My wife rushed home early from work. She gathered us in a family huddle and sternly but tenderly began by saying, "I don't know what the heck you two were thinking."

My thoughts are many. For one, back in the 1960s, if my parents had told me to "walk home by yourself" when I misbehaved, no one would have thought twice.

But what flew years ago doesn't fly today. I could have exposed my son to grave danger. I do know that. But in the moment of anger, I didn't think clearly.

A few hours later, I called The Parenting Center in Fort Worth. The nonprofit center has shown families in Tarrant County how to succeed through classes, counseling and home case management for more than 30 years.

"I can relate," said Pat Borgfeldt, the education program manager, after I told her what happened. "Don't feel alone. We get calls like this all the time.

"Some parents are willing to talk about the mistakes they make, and they recognize those mistakes. There are very few people who parent perfectly. We've all had those days where we don't like what we did. But learning from our mistakes is so important."

I asked what to do when, not if, we get in a standoff again. She said that in a power struggle with a child, a parent should never take it

*personally. A parent must quickly brainstorm pos-
sible solutions and choose the best one. Children
watch how we handle ourselves, and they learn
from that.*

*"Conflict and anger are good signs," she said.
"It's a natural part of a relationship. It's not bad
to be angry. It's what you do with that anger that
you need to take a look at."*

How do I do that? I asked.

*"Take a step back. Calm yourself. It's those
moments when we're so stressed and frustrated
that we say things that we can't take back. Once
they're out there, they are always out there. Learning good communications skills is so important
for parents."*

*Taking that step back, I now am grateful to the
other adults at the restaurant who took responsibility for the care of my son—and acted more
adult than I did. I am grateful to the police officers who handled the situation with care and
responsibility.*

*I hope my son and I learned from the experience.
We both have to calm down and learn to love and
live with each other better.*

A sidebar showed what parents can do:

*In moments of anger, The Parenting Center sug-
gests these steps in dealing with children in a
power struggle.*
  *• Identify the problem. Ask yourself, "What is
    making me angry?"*

- *Recognize signs that you are getting tense —tightened jaw, tense neck, anxiousness, irritability.*
- *Quickly think through possible solutions. Take a deep breath. Step back. Count to 10. Lower your voice.*
- *Communicate to the children with "I" language, rather than "You" language. For example, a parent can tell a child, "I am frustrated because... "*
- *Tell the child that the behavior is inappropriate. Listen to his or her complaint and acknowledge: "I hear you. Thanks for sharing." Statements like that can de-escalate a power struggle.*

The column ran the next day. Reaction was tepid. Readers commented at the bottom of the story that Austin should have been spanked. Others said they didn't believe it was the right of a government to get involved in parenting. Not a lot of people noticed—or cared—about what happened to us that day.

Not yet, at least.

There was a knock on the door. Two smiling women from Texas Child Protective Services. *Surprise!*

I wasn't ready. "Let me put my shirt on."

My two sons, Jonathan, then 23, and Austin, were upstairs.

I welcomed them to the living room, the formal room in the house that nobody sits in except for holidays. "OK, let's have a seat. What's your name?"

"Sylvia."

"And yours?"

"Molly."

They asked me to tell them what happened at McDonald's. I asked if they had seen the newspaper column. Both answered yes.

"And you just got up and left?" asked Molly, who got to the point.

"Yes."

"I guess there were some concerns because some

of the bystanders said he was trying to get in the car with you. And so obviously they were concerned that he could have been hit, that he could have tripped and fallen. About how long were you gone for?"

"Probably nine minutes."

"Just go drive around the block?"

"I drove up the road and then drove back down. Got caught at the light. Turned around, and that was it."

"OK. By the time you got back everything had sort of broken loose a little bit. You know, we obviously deal with far more serious stuff than this. But we have to address it. This is serious."

"I'm not minimizing it," I said.

"Every parent uses the 'I'm-going-to-leave-you-here-and-go-around-the-block trick' with their kids. But obviously, the concern here is mainly pulling the car doors; if something had happened, he would have been injured. I read your article. I know that you realized you made a mistake, and it won't happen again. It's just more of a precautionary thing."

"I understand. I know you have to come."

"Yeah, we do have to come. People don't always understand that. We try to be as easy as we can be on some of these things."

I tried to put them at ease: "You don't have to explain it. I get it. I'm glad you're here."

At that moment, I was glad. They go into households where children are beaten, not given proper food, clothing and medicine, security—or hope.

Somebody needs to take care of the little ones who need the most help and love.

"I appreciate that," Molly said. "I appreciate your making it easy."

"Either you or your wife have a criminal history?"

"No."

"Mental health problems?"

"No."

"These are all things I like to hear," she said. "Any domestic violence?"

"No."

"That's probably basically everything I need." She paused, then said, "This came in as physical abuse and neglect. Physical abuse because he could have been harmed, and neglect because he was left. I know it was probably a humbling experience to explain your position in the newspaper." She added, "We're not quite as scary as people think we are."

She paused. "If you don't mind, we'll just talk to Austin."

"OK."

Austin came down. I went upstairs. But I could hear what he and Molly were saying.

"Hi, Austin. I'm here to make sure you're safe. This is sort of a formality."

They talked about his school, baseball, our dog, video games and TV. Then she asked what happened.

"I was acting up. We went out to breakfast, and we were done. And I was like, 'Dad, can we please go?' He said no, he was reading the paper. I said, 'Dad, can we please go?' He wanted me to sit at a table, about three feet away. He wanted me to chill and everything. He said, 'No.' We dashed out to the car.

"He went in the car. I thought he was going to go like 10 feet, and he would come back, and I would learn my lesson. He was gone for seven or eight minutes."

"Is it usual or unusual?"

"Sometimes, he overreacts. Sometimes."

"Parents can do that," she said.

"So what happens when you get in trouble?"

"Well, the other day, we were playing a game, stoopball. We were tossing the ball off the wall. I thought he was cheating. He wasn't. So we got into it and everything. 'Dad, please can we just start over?' 'No, I'm going to go inside.' I said, 'Dad, please!' And he went inside."

"When you were chasing after the car and trying to get back in the car, were you ever scared you were going to, like, fall?"

"No, because I wasn't going to go much further."

"Do you usually get grounded or spanked or your stuff taken away?"

"I get my stuff taken away. Sometimes I get my PlayStation taken away."

"So what did you and your dad talk about afterward?"

"We need to take responsibility, which I did. We need to be more patient."

"Are you ever, like, really scared of your dad?"

"No."

"What about your mom?"

"Well, my mom, she deals with it really well. She says, 'Go take a chill timeout. Go up to your room for your five minutes.' Sometimes I go, 'Oh, Mom, please, Mom.' I go upstairs. 'If I'm good, can I please come out?' She says, 'OK, now 10 minutes.' The other week I took a nap."

"A real chill-out time," Molly said. "I think your dad knows that he didn't handle it the best way. My job is to check on you and make sure you get comfortable. Every kid gets in arguments with their parents. Thanks, Austin. I appreciate talking to you."

When I came down, she said, "You've got a cute son. He's cracking me up."

I wasn't laughing. They got up to leave. I let them out the door, then watched through the screen door as they walked to their car. At that moment, I felt a stab of fear. I realized that based on what they see and hear in these few minutes they can recommend that my son—any son or daughter—leave a home and enter protective foster care. They do it every day.

At first, I didn't realize when the caseworker spoke to me that she was using legal language when she said: "This came in as physical abuse and neglect. Physical abuse because he could have been harmed and neglect because he was left."

Ten days after the visit from the caseworkers, I got a phone message from Watauga Police Chief Rande Benjamin, the fifth chief in the 15 years I had lived in the neighborhood. I knew Benjamin from interviewing him on a story or two. He would never look me in the eye. I called back.

"Chief Benjamin."

"Hey Rande, this is David Lieber."

"Hey David. Got some bad news for you."

"What?"

"I have two arrest warrants for you that came through the DA's office — your case that you had at McDonald's. It got forwarded to the DA's office. This is not us. This is the DA's office. They reviewed the case. And we have two warrants for you.

"First one is for abandoning and endangering a child with criminal negligence. It's a felony [level] 4 which is a step below a state jail felony. The second one is for abandoning a child with intent. That's the same thing. A felony 4. Both fines are $2,000 apiece. What I'm doing is—this is a professional courtesy. I don't want you to have to get arrested or anything. So what I would say is contact your lawyer, OK?"

"Yeah."

"I'll give you 72 hours. That's till Friday, I guess. I don't have a problem till Friday. Either you can go to Tarrant County and turn yourself in. Get yourself some bonds. Or you can come down here, and I'll walk you through and get you out as quickly as possible. You can have your attorney call me if he needs any information on it. All right?"

Chief Rande Benjamin

Star-Telegram/Kelley Chinn

"All right. Bye. Thanks."

I called my wife, then my boss.

"Oh, my god," my wife said.

The boss at the newspaper listened and told me she was very sorry for me. Then she said she had to hang up and tell the executive editor.

CITATION AND
COMPLAINT

0004

Ticket #4 — City Manager
Who Hates People

Years before.

Bill Keating, the city manager who held the title of honorary police chief, decides to quit and move to the country. He's the gun-carrying city manager who slammed the newspaper on his desk not long after I arrived.

I write a column about his departure.

Bill Keating is a grumpy man. He hardly smiles in public. Bags underline his fierce eyes. And he's quick to temper.

Keating is the city manager of Watauga. He has run the city for a decade. Councils come and go, but Keating stays on. Old-school guy. Former Fort Worth policeman. Doesn't walk away from a fight.

Now he's a burnout.

"I got to where I hated people, and that's not good for a public servant," he says. "That's not good."

Keating is quitting, I write, so he can launch a country restaurant. A new career. A fresh start in a little town about an hour's drive north of Watauga. So I visit him there, in Forestburg, Texas, another speed-trap town. His new restaurant is the only one on Montague County's main road for 40 miles. Inside, he has decorated a wall with an old Texas flag. Tablecloths are classic red-and-white checkered. A pair of lucky horseshoes hang above the door. Things are looking good for the grump.

"The people here are genuine," Keating says. "A handshake still makes an agreement. A car breaks down? Everybody stops. You don't see that down there."

A century before, Keating's ancestors, Jeremiah and Mary Keating, bought 200 acres in what became Watauga. When Bill Keating returned to the town to build a career in city government, his strong ways enabled him to become the heart and soul of the town. "The whole city was used to answering to him, right down to the city council and mayor, all of them," a city council member once said. Good or bad, the town walked as Keating did. Now Keating wanted no more part of it.

CITATION AND COMPLAINT

0005

Ticket #5 — Ranking Officer Accused of Cover-up

A woman driving through a school zone in Watauga witnesses a man in a blue pickup driving beside her. He is masturbating. She writes down his license plate number and calls Watauga police.

Police arrest him and charge him with disorderly conduct. Usually, the charge for this crime is indecent exposure, a more serious offense. The woman's husband protests. He contacts me and complains. He's not like the usual angry husband. He is a police detective in an adjacent city. Coincidentally, Detective Jayson Steele also serves on a gang task force with Watauga officers.

Not for long.

In my column, I quote the angry detective complaining that Watauga police Lt. Bill Crawford, who handled the investigation, engaged in "substandard work" and "absolute incompetence." He says Watauga police orchestrated a cover-up. Strong language from a fellow cop.

Watauga Police Chief Eddie Hargroves promises to investigate. Eventually, the charge against the man is increased to indecent exposure. The detective/husband wins. But then he loses.

Chief Hargroves calls Steele a "loose cannon." He demands that Steele be removed from the joint police gang unit because he doesn't want his officers working with him. Steele is ordered to leave the unit.

I tell readers this story and add: "If that's true, maybe we need more loose cannons."

0006   CITATION AND COMPLAINT

Ticket #6 — The Cherry
Red Suburban

After my plea to readers to help Officer Woolbright, the man who was suspended without pay for sheltering the abused girl, dozens of gifts pour into the Watauga Police Department. The city sends them all back.

Each rejected donor also receives a letter from the department: "The city understands your actions in sending Officer Woolbright a check for $50. However, we must return the check to you because a city employee cannot receive or accept gratuities for special treatment related to job function. ... This applies to all city employees."

The reader who receives this note tells me, "The city doesn't have a heart." So I write in the newspaper:

> *I'm here to prove otherwise.*
>
> *Yes, dear readers, the city of Watauga does indeed have a big heart. The city policy doesn't really apply to all employees.*
>
> *The City Council recently decided to award a truly magnificent gift to City Manager Lee Maness.*
>
> *A 1997 Chevrolet Suburban.*
>
> *Color? Cherry red.*
>
> *Cost under a five-year lease-purchase? $33,822.*
>
> *Monthly payments to be paid by Watauga tax-payers? $665.13.*
>
> *OK, so technically, the cherry red Suburban is not a gratuity or a gift. It's a salary benefit, a bonus, a job perk for the city manager.*
>
> *The cherry red Suburban—henceforth known as the Watauga-mobile—will be owned by the city. But upon its delivery in a few months, the Watauga-mobile becomes the city manager's vehicle for*

business and personal use.

Lucky guy. Maness gets what he calls the ultimate "Texas pickup truck." The invoice says: gray leather, high-back bucket seats with AM/FM stereo, cassette and compact disc.

Who says Watauga doesn't have a heart?

Maybe Maness will give Woolbright the first ride in the Watauga-mobile. ...

He also gets to replace the 1992 Mitsubishi Diamante station wagon. ... "It's hard to get the bigger councilmen in it comfortably," Maness explained. "The leg space is not enough. You know, I've got some councilmen well over 6 feet."

The big need for the Watauga-mobile, Maness explained, will be to "showcase" the remaining 10 percent of undeveloped land to developers.

Councilman Lee Griffin explained, "If you show up in a Volkswagen Rabbit, how impressive are you going to be to some corporate executive?"

This is a city that shows no appreciation for a kind and caring public-safety officer who sheltered a beaten child.

But Watauga shows great appreciation for a rookie city manager by awarding him the cherry red Watauga-mobile.

Watauga is 4 square miles in size. Yet somehow, a station wagon isn't good enough because the council members are too big?

In their legs?

Or in their heads?

For years, whenever I wrote a column about Watauga that was critical, that displayed New York-style journalism, friends would crack the same joke: "Don't speed through Watauga."

Now that phrase had a different meaning. After the police chief told me I had until Friday to turn myself in, I worked to find a lawyer. I asked a lawyer I admired if he would take the case.

"I'm not a criminal lawyer, and you need a criminal lawyer. You need a lawyer with clout. This is serious."

"How serious?"

"Pretty damn serious."

"Why?"

"Well, I think there is a bent, a mentality right now in the prosecutorial world that child cases get treated very seriously. I think you have to treat it very seriously as a result of that."

"Who do you recommend?"

"Tim Moore."

Moore is a heavy-hitter in the county courthouse. A guy with the right connections who came up through the system. University of Texas graduate. Former assistant district attorney. Favorite of many courthouse judges. And most important, a solid criminal defense lawyer by reputation. The headlines from some of his cases represent a group of people you wouldn't want to meet at a law firm reunion:

GUNMAN GUILTY IN THREE SLAYINGS
MAN WHO KILLED STUDENT GETS 55 YEARS
SLAYING CONVICTION IS MAN'S SECOND
TEEN GETS 12 YEARS IN PLEA BARGAIN

I called Moore's office. Waited on hold for what seemed like a long time. My mind was frozen. I didn't

Lawyer Tim Moore

know what to think, what to tell him or what he would say. Although I had covered hundreds of court cases as a journalist, I had never been involved in one. Twenty years before, I hired a divorce lawyer, and before that, a real estate lawyer when I bought a house. In small claims court, once, I represented myself. That's my personal involvement in our legal system.

"Hey, Mr. Moore, this is David Lieber."

"Hi, David."

"I have a problem and I need your help."

I told him up front what I did for a living.

"OK, I knew I saw that name somewhere."

Told him about the incident and the column I wrote later for the newspaper. Told him about the police and their witness statements.

"The Watauga police chief just called me. He said there's a warrant out for my arrest for child endangerment and child abandonment."

"OK."

"I've written critically about the Watauga Police Department going back 15 years. I've got a slew of stories. When they stopped me, they called in the shift supervisor. I'm kind of a political being here in this one. I've let my boss know at the paper. And this is real serious for me because I'm about to be fingerprinted and get my mug shot taken. This could make the news, you know, all papers, all TV. I don't know how far it's going to go."

The lawyer took charge. "Here's what we need to do." He said he would take me on a "walk-through" downtown at the county courthouse. We'd go to a bond desk and then surrender.

"They fingerprint you and take your picture right there in the lobby so you don't even have to go into custody," he said.

He said he would call the police chief and find out what was going on. Before he hung up, I asked about something that was bothering me. I was the volunteer adviser for the student newspaper where Austin goes to school. Our newspaper had 60 children, and I worried how this would look: Mr.

Lieber from the student newspaper, accused of child abandonment and endangerment. I worried this would bring this joyful project of mine—turning out a 40-page newspaper every month that was mailed to the entire town the school was situated in—to an early end.

"I feel like I should call the head of this school right now," I said.

Moore said I could make the call but give few details.

"Because you don't need to talk to anybody about this, OK?"

"Well, my big boss at the paper wants to be apprised."

The lawyer said he would talk to the big boss for me because if I spoke to him, my boss could be called as a witness. I didn't realize it at the time, but this would cause me a problem. My big boss doesn't like it when his employees "lawyer up" and can't talk to him.

There would be a price to pay for that.

Americans struggle with parenting as much as we struggle with anything else in our lives—finances, jobs, marriage—maybe more. It's easy to forget that every generation of humanity, going back thousands, nay tens of thousands of years, has, during its turn, anguished about how to control the kids. The problems haven't changed. Gangs. Bad habits. Laziness. I'm sure it was no better in 20 B.C. when Cicero was giving it to Cicero Jr. Same issues. *Go to bed on time. Do well in school. Treat people right.* Actually, Cicero's kid was named Marcus, and, of course, when his father sent him to study with another philosopher friend to broaden Junior's horizons, the kid crapped out. "Away from his father's vigilant eye," historian H.J. Haskell explains, the son's major task was to "eat, drink and be merry." (And I picked Cicero at random.)

Today, though, the kid who won't listen is the norm, not the exception. The rebellious child who won't clean his room, who talks back, disobeys, shirks chores, gets in your face and acts with a sense of entitlement is Modern Boy. Ask any school teacher.

Gather a group of 21st century parents, and if they speak candidly, they will share similar stories from inside their family rooms of sudden, unexplained outbursts from their young rebels without a cause. Actually, though, it's not so different from when I was a boy. Baby boomers came of age when rebellion against parents was cool. Although I fantasized about a Ward and Beaver Cleaver relationship with my new son, I understood that wouldn't be possible. For us '50s and '60s kids, Mr. Cleaver was an early  role model, a black-and-white TV dad who looked good in a sweater, never screamed at his sons and got involved only when he had to. But we live in a color-TV world. My generation of baby boomers, and the one that followed us, didn't produce a lot of Ward Cleavers. That detached dad who stepped in on only the big problems was replaced by the yuppies (Young Urban Professionals) of my generation, who thoroughly and intentionally redefined parenting. Yuppies were determined to get involved in every possible aspect of their children's lives. And so we overdid it with the best schools, the best tutors, the best youth leagues. If we could afford it, the kids got it. Our children had to have the best of everything.

The generation of parents that followed is no better, maybe worse. Some do their kids' homework. They won't believe teachers who say their children misbehave. They yell too loudly at umpires and referees at their children's sporting events. If Ward Cleaver were a parent today, he'd push Beaver onto a "select" sports team, provide him with athletic equipment costing thousands of dollars, force him to take the college boards while in middle school to see how he stacks up, and buy him a new car on his 16th birthday.

We created a status culture aimed at adults, but the marketers targeted our children, too. Until federal law changed in 2010, almost any student who ventured onto a college campus was offered a credit card by companies that set up booths on the college green and offered free T-shirts. The status culture was very attainable, plus 20 percent interest.

In 2009, *Time* magazine's Nancy Gibbs wrote a cover story titled "The Growing Backlash Against Over-Parenting: Why Moms and Dads Need to Cut the Strings." She wrote of a new revolution aimed at rolling back "the almost comical overprotectiveness and overinvestment of moms and dads."

"The insurgency goes by many names—slow parenting, simplicity planning, free-range parenting —but the message is the same," she wrote. "Less is more; hovering is dangerous; failure is fruitful. You really want your children to succeed? Learn when to leave them alone. When you lighten up, they'll fly higher. We're often the ones who hold them down."

Over-parenting is so common because it's hard to say no to our kids. We not only love our children, we've become friends with them, and when we try to instill some sense of discipline that reminds us of the way parenting used to be, or we thought used to be, we don't get very far. Ask any parent how things are going and you often get the same answer: *My kid is killing me.*

In Latin, *parens* can be translated as a procreator, a father, a mother, a parent. A related verb—pareo—means to obey. Solomon's Proverbs 19:18 advises, "Chastise your son while there is hope for him, but be careful not to flog him to death. A man's ill temper brings it owns punishment." Proverbs 29:17 states, "Correct your son, and he will be a comfort to you and bring you delights of every kind."

Today, striking a balance between disciplining and loving a child is challenging. We're constantly trying to figure it out. Sometimes the roles of parents and children have switched. The kids are in charge, but the parents don't know it. Actor Peter Ustinov writes in his autobiography that parents are "the bones on which children sharpen their teeth."

Modern parenting is such a controversial topic that it's sometimes best to avoid in polite company. Yet it's hard *not* to talk about our kids. Our children are the center of our universe. We worship God, money and our children, not necessarily in that order. Our culture is so pro-child that the following conversation, which takes place in the British play *Otherwise Engaged* by Simon Gray, seems inconceivable in our children-come-first culture:

Stephen: What have you got against having children?

Simon: Well, Steve, in the first place there isn't enough room. In the second place they seem to start by mucking up their parents' lives, and then go on in the third place to muck up their own. In the fourth place it doesn't seem right to bring them into a world like this. In the fifth place and in the sixth place I don't like them very much in the first place. OK.

In "Bad Parents," a 2007 story in *Philadelphia* magazine, writer Tom McGrath states the case perfectly:

A generation of kids who've been overindulged, overprotected and generally over-parented seem to be overwhelmingly underprepared to live in the real world. .... How did this happen? How is it that a group of moms and dads who love their kids so much, and who were so intent on being great at raising them, has turned out to be, arguably, the worst parents ever? The short answer might be expressed like this: We've been too uptight about things— achievement, success, appearances—we should have been relaxed about, and too relaxed about things—values, integrity—that we should have been more uptight about. ... What's fascinating is that while many of us over-parent when it comes to promoting achievement, we under-parent when it comes to things parents prior to us were fanatical about for centuries: manners, courtesy, respect, responsibility. It's not that we're pro-brat, but that we're so uncomfortable being figures of authority that we can't demand those things of our kids. ...

Where our parents told us that yanking the cat's tail was wrong, we opt for the less judgmental "That's not a good choice, sweetie." Where our parents were content with "Because I said so," we feel compelled to explain our reasoning, lest we seem dictatorial. ... On one level, we may have decided that childhood is too important to be left to children, but on another, more important level, the kids are very much in charge.

If there's a leader of the movement to calm hyper-tense parents and convince them to ease up, it's Lenore Skenazy. If you Google "America's Worst Mom," her name and story come up page after page. Ske-

Lenore Skenazy

nazy is the self-proclaimed "Generalissimo of the Free-Range Kids Movement." Part of her quest has been to bring attention to governmental authorities who intervene in parent-child cases where, maybe, their attention is unnecessary.

Skenazy backed into this movement by accident. She wrote a column for the *New York Sun* newspaper confessing that she let her 9-year-old son ride the New York City subway alone for the first time. "I knew he was ready, so I let him go," she explains in her book *Free-Range Kids: How to Raise Safe, Self-Reliant Children (Without Going Nuts With Worry)*. She handed him a subway map, a transit card for free rides, $20 in case of an emergency and some quarters to make a phone call. When she told people about it later, many were horrified.

After the column was published, she was asked to appear on NBC's *Today* show. She and her son Izzy told their story to morning viewers. Then in the next segment, a parenting expert weighed in and called her horrible. It made for great TV. When her segment was over, MSNBC called. They wanted her. Fox News called, too.

"And suddenly, weirdly, I found myself at that place you always hear about: the center of a media storm," she writes. "It was kind of fun, but also kind of terrifying—because everyone was weighing in on my parenting skills. Reporters queried from China, Israel, Australia, Malta. Newspapers, blogs, magazines, even the BBC."

At first, the title of "America's Worst Mom" bothered her. "That's not what I am," she says. But she saw her chance to influence others, and she seized it. She appeared on ABC's *The View*, and nobody on the panel took her side. Yet she insists that she's onto something and refuses to give up. "I feel like parents are taking away some of the main ways that children do get safe, which is by feeling confident, which is by knowing their own way around, which is by interacting with people they don't know and getting to know the neighbors and feeling confident around them," she told a reporter for the *Cape Cod Times*. "The safe kids are the confident kids, and the confident kids are the ones who've been doing things on their own."

Or put another way, she says: "The way kids learn to be resourceful is by having to use their resources."

Skenazy launched a blog and a fun Twitter feed @FreeRangeKids. Nearly every day, she posts links and insights into the movement, which she describes this way on the Free-Range Kids blog: "Do you ever let your kid ride a bike to the library? Walk to school? Make dinner? Or are you thinking about it? If so, you are raising a Free-Range Kid! Free-Rangers believe in helmets, car seats, seat belts—safety! We just do not believe that every time school-age kids go outside, they need a security detail."

She offers an Outrage of the Week. ("Hi Readers, I'm sorry to say this is happening in my town, New York City: Seven chess players have to appear in court for playing the game of kings on the stone chess tables close to a playground—a playground where adults are forbidden unless they are accompanied by a child. Because, of course, any human anywhere NEAR a child who isn't personally taking care of one MUST be a monstrosity. Except these particular monstrosities quietly play chess together.

Have for years. They even teach the local kids how to play. Terrifying!")

When her blog was named the "Most Controversial" mommy blog by parenting website Babble, Skenazy tweeted, "Cool! (Even tho I don't think I AM controversial.)"

In a 2010 *Wall Street Journal* column, she poked fun at parent car lines at school. Only 1 in 10 students bike or walk home from school anymore, even though the national crime rate has dropped. Crimes against children are rare enough; that's why the exceptions make news. She writes:

> When the [school] bell finally rings, the first car races into the pickup spot, whereupon the car-line monitor barks into a walkie-talkie: "Devin's mom is here!" Devin is grabbed from the gym, escorted to the sidewalk and hustled into the car as if under enemy fire. His mom peels out and the next car pulls up. "Sydney's mom is here!"...
>
> How did we get to this point? How did we forget that it's just a walk to school?
>
> Simple. We bought the line that good parenting is the same as over-parenting. That the more we could do for our children, the better. We forgot the joy of scuffing down the street when we were young, crunching leaves, picking up seeds, and decided we'd do it all for our kids, independence be damned!

None of this was on my mind that August day when I told Austin to sit down and shut up in that McDonald's. I love my children with all my heart. Yet I'm quite sure that in previous times, a boy ordered to walk home after an uproar in a public place would have walked home. Most likely, an older person would have said, "Son, you shouldn't act like that. Now get on home and apologize to your dad."

Now you call the cops.

I had no way of knowing, as I prepared to meet my new lawyer, that I would, in a few days, find myself at the center of a debate about the proper roles for parents, children and authorities in the disciplining of today's children.

Should police and prosecutors get involved? Or should parents be allowed to make their own decisions about how to rear their children? Does the government interfere too much? Do parents know how to do their jobs properly?

Lots of questions.

Why me?

Here are the two state statutes I was charged with violating:

Texas Penal Code, statute 22.041
ABANDONING OR ENDANGERING A CHILD

In state law, "abandon" means "to leave a child in any place without providing reasonable and necessary care for the child, under circumstances under which no reasonable, similarly situated adult would leave a child of that age and ability."

Count 1 Abandonment: A person commits an offense if, having custody, care or control of a child younger than 15 years, he intentionally abandons the child in any place under circumstances that expose the child to an unreasonable risk of harm.

Count 2 Endangerment: A person commits an offense if he intentionally, knowingly, recklessly, or with criminal negligence, by act or omission, engages in conduct that places a child younger than 15 years in imminent danger of death, bodily injury, or physical or mental impairment."

I began receiving solicitation letters from lawyers. Each lawyer offered his or her special pitch.

- "No case is too big or too small. We offer payment plans. Last year alone, of the five major federal drug cases, I defended four of them."
- "The outcome of your cases could impact the rest of your life. ... My fees are competitive and start at only $350."
- "All credit cards accepted."
- "Felony cases can be handled for as little as $250."
- "We have assigned your file a case number of 8026. It is urgent to call as soon as possible to discuss how you want to handle this case."
- "$200 Down gets me Fighting for You."

I stuck with Tim Moore. Karen and I waited in his outer office for our first meeting. When Moore came out to fetch me, he greeted Karen, then asked her to wait outside.

Inside, I told him everything I could think of. If Austin had walked home, he would have crossed a main street on a green light and then sailed through our neighborhood with a shortcut and be home in less than 15 minutes.

The police, they knew me because of my job. I had a history with them. The district attorney? A couple of times, I had written columns portraying his opponent's campaign in a positive light.

Moore told me he would do some research on my case and let me know what he found.

A few days later, Moore accompanied me to the courthouse for my walk-through. As a first-time offender, I qualified for reduced bail, but the catch was I'd never see the money again no matter how the case turned out. My requirement was that I check in once a month.

After that, I headed to the lobby for my mug shot and fingerprinting. A sheriff's deputy took my fingers and, one by one, rolled them across an electronic pad. No ink involved. He scanned my eyeballs, too. He did this without looking at me. Then it was time for the mug shot photo. I fretted about the photo. I didn't want to look like a killer. But the lighting wasn't good. That and my unintentional sour expression made for a creepy photo. I guess it's hard not to look guilty in a mug shot. When I saw the photo later—on the TV news—it scared me. I didn't like that guy at all.

Now it was official. I was arrested and booked. The district attorney would decide what to do next. Would my case go to a criminal grand jury?

But first I had to deal with what Lenore Skenazy called "the center of a media storm."

Thousands of times in 30 years as a newspaperman I had done it to other people. People I often never met. People whose stories I didn't know. People who couldn't tell me what happened because somebody else wouldn't let them. People whose names and problems I put in the newspaper anyway.

I never knew what that felt like until The Associated Press took the details that were reported in my own newspaper and spread them across the land.

COLUMNIST ACCUSED OF
LEAVING SON IN PARKING LOT

The Associated Press
Aug. 27, 2008

FORT WORTH, Texas — A *Fort Worth Star-Telegram* columnist is accused of leaving his 11-year-old son in a restaurant parking lot after an argument, Watauga police said.

Dave Lieber, 51, was arrested and turned himself in to the Tarrant County Jail on Tuesday, authorities said. He was released on $4,000 bail.

He was arrested on two probable cause warrants, one for child abandonment with intent to return and the other for child abandonment/ endangering a child, said Watauga police Detective Tiffany Ward. Both are felonies.

Police will refer the case to the Tarrant County district attorney, who will determine whether to file charges.

Lieber declined to comment on the advice of his attorney.

Police responded to a Watauga fast-food restaurant on Aug. 13 after a customer called 911 and reported an argument between a child and an adult, who had driven off while the boy was still in the parking lot, Ward said.

While police were interviewing witnesses, Lieber returned and was allowed to leave with his son, she said. But the case was forwarded to the Watauga police criminal investigation division.

The police report did not indicate how long the

boy was left at the restaurant, Ward said.

Lieber wrote about the incident in an Aug. 15 column, saying he regretted his actions. He said he was gone for "several minutes" before he returned to get his son.

"I made a stupid and quite serious mistake," Lieber wrote in his column.

Star-Telegram Executive Editor Jim Witt said Lieber would be suspended from writing "The Watchdog" column, which investigates consumer complaints, while the case moves through the judicial system.

"Then we'll have to see what the result is before we make any further decisions concerning this," Witt told the newspaper.

The Dallas Morning News story added more details:

"The act of backing the vehicle caused the child to bounce against the side of the vehicle while it was in motion," the affidavit said. "The child chased after the vehicle through the parking lot as it exited and drove away."

Watauga Police Chief Rande Benjamin said Mr. Lieber told them he drove away because he needed to cool off. He returned minutes later to retrieve his son, the chief said. ...

"We asked if he had been punched or if the vehicle hit him," Chief Benjamin said. The child said "he was fine, but we contacted CPS to put them on the case. He was not struck, and he was not endangered."

CPS spokeswoman Marisa Gonzales would not comment other than to say the boy is not in the agency's custody.

Police said Lieber was allowed to leave the restaurant with his son because the boy was traumatized.

Chief Benjamin said investigators have turned their probe over to the Tarrant County district attorney's office. A spokesman for the office said they are awaiting a formal package from police.

On news radio station KRLD-AM, the announcer said:

The Watchdog columnist for the *Fort Worth Star-Telegram*, Dave Lieber, is out on bail following his arrest on charges of child abandonment.

On the TV news, here were the headline stories: Hurricane Gustav heads toward Louisiana.

Barack Obama prepares to give his acceptance speech for the Democratic presidential nomination.

And mine.

Channel 8, Channel 11, Channel 5, Channel 4. They all covered it.

At KDFW Fox 4 News reporter Natalie Solis put a business card inside my screen door. Then she and her satellite truck planted themselves at Watauga police headquarters for live remotes for the newscasts at 5 p.m. and 6 p.m. Then there was a shift change and reporter Lari Barager moved the truck up the street to McDonald's for the 9 p.m. and 10 p.m. newscasts.

My lawyer said I couldn't comment. All I could do was listen to their live broadcasts.

Solis began, "This is a story that's generating lots of discussion. On one side, parents say they can understand how other parents may lose their cool. On the other side, parents say you should never leave a child alone. Add into that the person we are talking about is in the public eye. Dave Lieber, who has been writing for the *Star-Telegram* for the last 15 years. ..."

She reported that the distance to my home was 1.5 miles (actually half with shortcuts through the neighborhood for walkers). She showed my creepy mug shot. The caption under the mug shot was erroneous, yet fitting considering the stupidity of my mistake. For each of the four Fox broadcasts, the caption gave me a new nickname:

DAVIE LIEBER.

There was an on-the-street interview. A woman said, "We all make mistakes as a parent."

The reporter asked, "Do you think he should face charges?"

"No, I think that's ridiculous. I think he's a good dad. I know him. I see him out playing with him, and all the other activities he's had with his child have been appropriate and wonderful and loving."

The woman who said this, Claudia Rivera, has lived across the street from me for more than a decade. Nice testimonial. Small world. Thank you, neighbor.

Chief Benjamin was interviewed. He said, "The officers called and asked what I would do, and I told them what is best for the child is to let him go home with the dad. We'll report it to CPS and make the case to the district attorney and make sure we have a strong case."

The reporter concluded, "What makes this case different are other factors: the witnesses, the child trying to get into a vehicle as it moved away, and they said the fact that Lieber then wrote about it, in essence, admitting to abandoning the child. Further bolstering their case in getting those arrest warrants."

When Solis' report was finished, anchor Steve Eager asked, "I know Natalie this is touchy for everyone. How long did this play out? Do we know?"

She answered, "I don't know exactly how long this whole thing did play out. ... There was one discrepancy in the column. He says he was gone for several minutes before he came back. According to the arrest warrant affidavit, it was more like 15. So how long this entire thing—the time it took for it all to transpire? A bit unclear. But we do know there was a bit of time there that he was away from the McDonald's. And, of course, that is now what has led to these charges."

The next day, a producer for another TV show called. They wanted to interview me. I declined. Later, when I told my wife that *Inside Edition* was interested, she didn't believe me.

"You're kidding."

"I'm not."

When strangers looked curiously upon the scarlet letter,—and none ever failed to do so, —they branded it afresh into Hester's soul; so that, oftentimes, she could scarcely refrain, yet always did refrain, from covering the symbol with her hand. But then, again, an accustomed eye had likewise its own anguish to inflict. Its cool stare of familiarity was intolerable.

— Nathaniel Hawthorne
The Scarlett Letter

They hated me.

Blogs in America and around the world picked up the story. Comments were publicly posted by the hundreds. Opinions about me cascaded across cyberspace. I spent an hour each day reading them.

batarina: What an idiot!!!!!!!!!!!!

c: Leaving a child alone in a restaurant is not an appropriate form of punishment by any means. In this day and age, eleven years old is not old enough to be left alone, anywhere!!! Children that age are kidnapped and murdered every day.

Don't throw stones if you live in glass houses: Hopefully this experience will cause him to think before opening his big mouth and keeping his big nose out of places it has no business in. You go CPS!!! Nail him with all you can. There is no one I can think of that is more deserving.

EXPAT: The image of a child trying to open his parent's car door while it is driving away is abandonment, pure and simple.... What if it was at night? Lieber was wrong. It WAS abandonment!

sanlivette: I hope Mrs. Lieber kicked the crap out of her husband.

Matt: The dad sounds like an obnoxious jerk. My dad was a cop. He's had his fill of dead kids. If they have to come down on a harmless dolt to make a point, so be it.

Jeff: I don't understand something. What is a father doing arguing with his 11-year-old son? Arguing! Who's the dad here anyway? A dad lays down the law. The 11-year-old complies. Period. This should have been established in toddlerhood. It shouldn't even occur to the kid that he can argue his dad into leaving the restaurant before he's finished eating. The lost art of parenting.

Alicia: Frankly, throwing someone out of a car, even if it's not moving, or driving away in anger and abandoning them, for however short a time, is an abusive act.

pentamom: This guy is obviously completely incompetent as a father.

Mike: Mr. Lieber was a jerk, because as a parent

your job is to supervise your 11-year-old, not throw up your hands and say, "I'm out of here."

Matt: I do know that it's a mile or more from Lieber's house to the restaurant, not "a few blocks," and I tend to think that when a self-righteous turd like Lieber is lying about one aspect of his story, he's probably lying about other parts of it.

TechLaw01: Surely you see what a piece of ---- you are? Surely you know when you parent a child it becomes about them and not you. I dread the reports that will air when you parent him as a teen. Grow up. Step back from the mirror. Focus on your child. Spend some one-on-one time and see what benefits you reap from ACTUALLY paying attention to him. God bless him.

Savannah: The biggest, most important job of a parent is to ensure the SAFETY and WELL-BEING of their child(ren) to the best of their ability.... It was irrational, and it was his fault. A parent does not allow a child to control them. A parent must be rational and responsible, even when a child is not. The bottom line here is that laws were broken whether you agree with those laws or not.

Queen Bee: I'm surprised CPS hasn't removed the child from the home. Seriously.

gdunham: Are you in jail now? good! Smug bully

doesnt always work does it? wahh,wahh,wahh. What a dip ----.

ThomasM: Don't you know nothing will EVER be the same between you and your son, you fool?

And many more.

Fortunately for my tattered ego, a much higher percentage of Internet posters were sympathetic.

Richard: Hell, my mom did that to me when I was about 10-11 years old. I am in my 60s now. Taught my happy butt a lesson!! Hope this kid learns as well.

Cro Magnum Man: The only ones who should be facing criminal prosecution in this case are the people at McDonald's who called the police, and the police and DA who were stupid enough to act on that call. ... It is not YOUR business, or mine, how Mr. and Mrs. Muckenfuss down the street raise little Buford and his sister. It's THEIR business. Not yours. Not the courts. Not anyone's. The ONLY time it becomes our business is when they are hurting them beyond what is considered normal in life, such as rape, physical injury beyond a smack in the chops or other forms of abuse.

Catherine: How stupid! The child is plenty old enough under Texas law to be at a fast food restaurant by himself. The father told him to meet him at home. He wasn't abandoning him. If they call this abandonment, all the latch-key kids who have to walk home after school should be in CPS custody, too.

C.Asada: Criminal charges? Seriously?

Jen: Abandonment??? Dave was parenting his out-of-control son. Teaching him a lesson is what he was doing. Dave seemed like he was trying to use "tough-love" technique on his son and for doing that he got slapped in the face.

Ron Williams: Let the guy parent his boy! … Maybe there was some bad judgment, but it was from the police.

Mercie: I wonder if this guy is somehow disliked because of his "Watchdog" column. Perhaps he is being singled out and charged for a reason other than trying to punish for what sounds like non-felonious conduct. This is absurd.

Joe: As a young parent myself I believe I have some "old-school" qualities. I definitely think that this father did not do anything wrong. I know of 2 separate occasions that my father did the same thing to me. As long as there was no interstate to cross and the path home was not forbidding, the father should not face charges at all. Police need to be supportive, not interfering, of parental discipline—especially when it helps prevent them from needing handcuffs on a child later.

I heart Dave: Watauga police are corrupt. If they worked on half of their cases like they have on this one, maybe they could actually solve something.

chg: It's no secret that the Watauga City gov't has had it in for Dave Lieber for many years. His column has shaken them up (for the better!) many a time. The police ON THE SCENE released Dave and his son without incident because NOTHING HAPPENED. … Leave a stellar citizen like Dave Lieber to his own, self-admitted guilt. He has been contrite and forthcoming from the beginning, voluntarily! We need MORE Dave Liebers in this community.

D: Has to be more to the story. Has to. A 5th grader can walk a few blocks without the cops being called.

Reagan: This is probably karma biting Lieber in the rear. He has pissed somebody off in the Watauga DPS and they wanted a little payback.

0007

CITATION AND
COMPLAINT

**Ticket #7 — Police Chief
Has Love Child**

Years before.

The Watauga police chief, Eddie Hargroves, has come up through the ranks. Now he is at the center of a highly sensitive personnel dispute. A Watauga policewoman, Liberty Spinella, files a complaint alleging sexual harassment and intimidation against the chief and three sergeants. I report her allegations.

In a strange sideshow to this matter, Spinella's complaint makes public something long rumored: that several years ago the married Hargroves had an affair with a woman in Watauga, resulting in a child.

At the time, the woman was dating another Watauga officer, Glenn Spinella.

After Liberty Spinella joined the force, she married Glenn Spinella, who remains a Watauga officer.

Liberty Spinella wrote in her complaint, "I am currently being scrutinized and harassed by Chief Hargroves because Chief Hargroves has a personal conflict of interest with Sgt. Spinella due to information Sgt. Spinella has regarding an illegitimate child of Chief Hargroves."

In an interview, Hargroves acknowledged the past relationship with the woman and said he has helped care for the child.

CITATION AND COMPLAINT

0008

Ticket #8 — Police
Department in Turmoil

Chief Hargroves is cleared of Spinella's allegations, but a consultant's report finds a lack of confidence in his leadership. Hargroves is forced to resign.

I describe the report's contents in the newspaper:

There is a severe lack of confidence by the employees in the current administration's ability to lead the department. ... The report charges that professional standards are not reviewed annually. Goals and objectives are not set as part of the planning and budget process. Employees' criminal history and driver's license records are not verified annually. Supervisors are not trained about how to conduct performance reviews.

Officers do not have their own policy manuals and were often not knowledgeable about department policies. Investigators do not have a system requiring all assigned cases to be reviewed and updated regularly.

The department lacks written emergency plans. Dispatchers have inadequate security inside the police station.

The jail, designed to temporarily hold prisoners, is used to keep prisoners locked up for longer periods of time. Yet there is no jail supervisor. A dispatcher on duty usually supervises prisoners. The consultant also found unsanitary conditions in the jail.

0009

CITATION AND
COMPLAINT

Ticket #9 — Chief's Handling of
Record-Keeping at Issue

I do more reporting and uncover one of the reasons Hargroves was forced out. The chief had learned that records in the fire department were fabricated and did nothing about it. The records were daily logs required to make sure that firefighters' air packs are checked each day. Only the records hadn't been kept properly for two years. Lt. Bill Crawford says he ordered the records, which are required by state law, to be re-created.

In two interviews, Hargroves and Crawford confirmed the allegations but called them a misunderstanding. No state regulations were broken, they insisted, because the state does not require the air packs to be checked every day. However, Watauga policy requires daily checks. ...

Crawford said, "I took the originals and I told [a firefighter], 'I want you to go back and make two pages of clean checks and this will start the clean book.'" ...

Here's my problem with Crawford's explanation: You shouldn't make things up in public records, especially, in this case, by backdating and pretending to know which officer did the air checks from two years ago. Who could remember? And these are government records, not somebody's diary.

00010 CITATION AND COMPLAINT

Ticket #10 — City Hall in Turmoil

In my column, I go for broke, calling for the ouster of several city council members and the city manager whom they support. Real New York-style journalism.

City Manager Lee Maness, he of the cherry red Watauga-mobile fame, had angered some in the town with his ideas and his domineering personality (not unlike predecessor Bill Keating). Maness wanted to build a new City Hall inside the bottom portion of the city's water tower. He wanted to partner with the city's largest

Baptist church, the one beside City Hall, on an unpopular land-sharing deal. He used his city secretary to handle his private business. And he hired his brother to perform city work.

> That's why the best hope for the future of Watauga, in my opinion, is a clean sweep. What's needed is a recall election of council members whose terms have not expired, combined with new council candidates running against those who are up for re-election.
> After a new council is installed, Watauga's new council can hire another city manager. ...
> Bring on the recall. Bring on a new slew of candidates. Most important, bring the people back to City Hall to take charge of what is rightfully theirs.

And that's exactly what happens. Two council members are recalled. New council members come in, and, very quickly, they fire Maness. At the tumultuous meeting where he is ousted, I watch as the action goes on past midnight. When the vote to fire the city manager is final, one of the recalled councilmen shouts at a new councilman: "Immature punk kid!" Then he yells at another, "You low-life tramp!"

> It was ugly, ugly, ugly.
> Watauga police had to escort the council members to their cars.
> "I've never witnessed so much animosity in my

life," Councilwoman Patty Tucker said. "Every comment was negative. Nobody wanted to make things happen for the city."

00011

CITATION AND COMPLAINT

Ticket #11 — Developer Hands Mayor Cash

A developer invites Watauga Mayor Harry Jeffries and several other area mayors to a luncheon. At the end of the luncheon, the developer, Bob Kohsmann, says to the mayors, "Congratulations, you won the door prize. Thanks for coming."

The developer hands each mayor an envelope. Inside is Kohsmann's business card and two crisp new $50 bills.

One of the mayors is upset about this gesture. He calls me and tells me about it. For my column, I call the mayors and ask them to tell me what happened and what they planned to do with the $100.

"I didn't know what was in the envelope," the Watauga mayor said in an interview. "I thought

it was just his business card and realized what it was when I got home. I didn't know what to think about it. I'm just going to donate it to the Watauga library."

Along that speed trap I mentioned are a police station, City Hall, the McDonald's and also the biggest Baptist church in town. No surprise, then, to learn that the church and I have history, too. There's something hazardous about that little stretch of Watauga roadway for me, I guess. My trouble zone.

Harvest Baptist Church's pastor was Ollin Collins, a tall, handsome, sandy-haired man with big ideas about God, a church and the people in it. He was one of the most ambitious preachers in

The church is across the street from the McDonald's.

Texas—and that's saying a lot. Absolutely he is one of the most charismatic men I ever met.

He started with a tiny neighborhood church and 20 years later, his dream was coming true. Across from McDonald's, he built a 3,150-seat worship hall. Why that capacity? Because his research showed that would make the sanctuary of his new $7 million Watauga megachurch the biggest auditorium in the county.

Collins was well-known among Southern Baptists. He was chairman of the board of Southwestern Baptist Theological Seminary, then the largest in the nation. He was on statewide television. He had plans to take his ministry national and worldwide, too.

Our relationship was like a bad road show. The Baptist preacher and the New York Jew. Comical at times, with high stakes for both of us. Alternately, he welcomed me, scolded me, made peace with me, wel-

Pastor Ollin Collins

comed me back to his services, ordered his ushers to kick me out, tried to get me fired, and once, tried to hire me as his PR agent. Eventually, the ground collapsed beneath him.

Collins—or his church, actually—was Watauga's largest landowner. Collins picked up most of the church's 82 acres at fire sale prices following the Texas savings and loan bust in the 1980s. ("God said one day, 'You better buy it if it's available.' So we studied, actually found out who to get in touch with, and they said, 'Make an offer.' And we did.") He called his congregants "guys" as in "Hey guys, stick with me." And I must give him credit for this:

he changed the lives of some of his congregants for the better.

However.

The preacher aimed to become Watauga's political boss. Only he didn't want anyone to know.

When the city threatened to seize some of the church's land for parkland, Collins grew incensed. He began recruiting and backing candidates for Watauga mayor and council. He recruited what his guys called "God thinkers" who would support him.

When his mayoral candidate knocked the incumbent mayor (the one who told his wife to be quiet) out of the race and headed into a runoff, the pastor's candidate triumphantly said, "The Christians in our community have spoken."

That's how Collins' secret leaked out. He had a slate of candidates. I wrote about what he was doing. In the election, his three candidates lost. Collins blamed me, saying the press exposure was the reason. He asked if I intended to keep writing about future candidates and their connection to his church. I said I would. So he came up with a different strategy (that I wrote about, too). He instructed his next set of God-thinkers running for office: "Don't go around telling people it's God's will to be elected. Don't campaign on the fact that you're a Christian."

During some of his Sunday sermons, especially on the Sundays when my stories about him were in the newspaper, Collins denounced me from the pulpit. He didn't like my reporting, he told his guys, but that wasn't the real problem. He informed them that I was Jewish, and I hadn't accepted Jesus as my lord and savior.

Before one election, he asked 250 Watauga residents who belonged to his church if they would remain after services for a private talk. In that talk, others told me later, he took me to task for writing about his candidates. Then he said something that was startling. Why hadn't Dave Lieber, he asked, "made a big deal over the Mormons trying to take over Watauga, instead of me trying to take over Watauga?" Whoa. The city manager was a Mormon as were two of the council members. When I asked Collins the next day what exactly he had said, he repeated his words for accuracy.

I remembered a message he placed years before on the church sign promoting his Sunday sermon: "Mormonism: Cult or Christian?" Collins was big on signs. He placed his face on large highway billboards. He looked like a movie star. In his church, he installed a tanning booth to attract new members, then placed a large sign on the church's exterior wall facing McDonald's. The sign announced "TANNING." Collins installed a hot tub inside his church, too.

Then, in 1998, five women came forward and accused Collins of abusing his position as church leader by having extramarital affairs. In court documents, the women described how they visited Collins for marital counseling. In return, Collins pressured them for sex. The documents charged that he engaged in sex acts in his church office, in the church foyer, in private residences, in parked cars and in hotel rooms while attending pastor conventions and seminary meetings. He lost his job, his reputation. Paul Harvey talked about him on the radio.

He bought a new business, Big O Bail Bonds, and also worked in real estate. Last I heard, after a decade in exile, he was back running a church about an hour's drive from his old one.

Before he left Watauga forever, though, he and the city manager, Maness, the one he fought with about the parkland, agreed on one thing. Collins and Maness made a trip to visit my top boss, Jim Witt. Both men made the case that I should be removed from my job or, at least, have some of my feathers plucked. But Witt, who was also in charge when I was arrested years later, didn't take their advice. Ultimately, the preacher was gone, and so was the city manager. I was still there. Driving up and down that strip every day. Not realizing that this little corner of the world would play a much larger role in my destiny.

I wasn't always a big troublemaker in Watauga. Sometimes, I was a civic booster. Driving through town every day, I saw parts of the city that I admired—and wrote about them in the newspaper. Watauga is only 4 square miles in area, a working-class community nestled next to Fort Worth, America's 16th largest city. Watauga is mostly overlooked. It lacks a central business core, and its chamber of commerce is headquartered in another city. The area high school is elsewhere, too. There's no Rotary Club, no women's club, no real force that could help the town move forward. But there's still a lot to admire about a place where the streets have patriotic names like Betsy Ross, Bunker Boulevard, Concord Street and Declaration.

I especially love the little church on the hillside, the oldest church building around. After the experience with Pastor Collins up the street, it was energizing to discover this treasure.

Far from crowded malls, from commercials for electric razors, from television evangelists seeking cash for Christmas, the little church on the prairie celebrated the holidays in a humble yet dignified way.

Watauga Presbyterian Church turned 130 years old on Sunday. The pioneer church is a blessing because it symbolizes a time before razzle-dazzle took over our lives.

It's possible, though, that this could be the last Christmas celebration for the little church on the prairie.

Dwindling membership means the church might not live up to the joyful words of the dedicatory prayer uttered 130 years ago on Dec. 14, 1867.

"May they always be aware of Thy sustaining power and be effective witnesses that cause Thy church to grow more and more."

Thy church might die.

The church endowment fund is running out. Word among the 15 active members is that the church could close sometime after the first of the year.

For more than a century, locals have climbed the steep hill beside White Branch Creek to worship in the plain white church decorated with two stained-glass windows, an old-fashioned ceiling fan and a painting of Jesus, whose eyes appear to follow you around the sanctuary.

There's no church staff or telephone. It's church the way church used to be.

I love the old history of the town. I was curious about the Great Watauga Train Wreck of 1918. There was a photo and an explanation in the town history display at City Hall. That's all I knew. I asked around about this momentous event in the town's history, and no one seemed to know any more. So I went downtown to the Fort Worth Public Library and searched the archives. I knew the train wreck occurred in the summertime because folks in the old photographs wore summer clothes. The newspapers were stored on microfilm rolls. First, I pulled the summer months for the two daily newspapers. On the creaky microfilm machine, I looked at every page of both newspapers for that summer of 1918. Learned a lot about World War I. But never saw a blip about the Great Watauga Train Wreck of 1918. OK, maybe it didn't happen in the summer. So I scrolled through every page of every issue of both newspapers. Jan. 1 to Dec. 31, 1918. Three hundred and sixty-five days times two newspapers. I turned the rusty handle on the microfilm machine and pages rolled past on a blurry, scratched screen. The microfilm squeaked loudly as the months flew by. Hundreds of days. Thousands of pages. But I couldn't find the train wreck. I grew dizzy. By the time I switched to the second daily paper, I felt nauseated. Never found what I was looking for in those newspapers. The dizziness lasted several days.

After that, I searched 1918 train records, wrote train history researchers and scoured the Internet. Members of the Watauga Historical Society couldn't help. Finally, I visited the Watauga library and explained my dilemma to the librarians. The librarians couldn't find anything either. Then librarian Connie Barnes gave it one more shot. She found the entire story of the train wreck. She called me triumphantly to let me know the news. Quickly, I asked her how she did it. "A lot of serendipity and just perseverance, really," she explained. Everyone was looking for the wreck of 1918. Turns out the wreck actually happened in 1917. Watauga history had it wrong.

I love my two favorite restaurants in town. Tony's Pizza and Pasta serves New York-style pizza by the slice (a rarity in many Texas pizza parlors). And I'm a big fan of the legendary Chef Point Cafe. Wrote the first major story on the gourmet restaurant situated in a gas station. That started an avalanche of TV, newspaper, magazine and online coverage that elevated the popular and unusual Watauga eatery to national fame.

And ... I met a man, Bill Ditman, who was a member of SERTOMA, a U.S. service club that gets its unusual name from its mission of Service To Mankind. Ditman was moving to Fort Worth and wanted to know if any area towns were in need of a service club. I talked to him about Watauga. About how the town had nothing to call its own. When he arrived, I introduced him to town leaders. Promoted the first meeting in the newspaper, too.

Today, years later, the SERTOMA Club of Watauga, Texas, is thriving. The club helps the disabled and the needy, sponsors a lecture series at the library and assists in other community projects. Watauga finally has its own service organization.

My newspaper career, 30 years in the making, appeared to be a week away from ending. The paper wasn't pulling the plug on me. I was the one that planned to call it quits. Felt as if I had no choice.

The decision by Executive Editor Jim Witt was that I would be put on inside duties. The Watchdog column would cease to run until the matter was cleared up in the courts. I would report to work each day and put in my eight hours helping everyone do their jobs. Maybe some copy editing or research or whatnot. The thought of that about killed me. I knew that the courts could take up to two years to sort things out.

Yet I supported Witt's decision 100 percent. He had the reputation of a proud, century-old newspaper to protect. I am not like other reporters on the paper. I'm The Watchdog. It looks terrible for your watchdog columnist to be writing about the shortcomings of others when he faces two criminal felony counts himself. Witt had no choice but to take the stance he did, especially since my lawyer wouldn't let him talk to me.

My other option was to take a voluntary buyout being offered to everyone in the company with a hefty financial package. The deadline was a week away. I made a decision: If, by the buyout deadline, my case was still unresolved, I was going to leave the newspaper, along with dozens of others taking the buyout. I couldn't sit still for months under what I considered to be newspaper house arrest.

Witt didn't make his decision in isolation. He was hearing from readers. One reader wrote, "I read with interest the article today concerning his arrest. I yelled loudly 'Thank God. Justice for the child.' This is what Dave deserves. I only hope the legal system does the right thing. This guy is not stable. Fighting with his child, blowing his stack, and then abandoning him at a McDonald's—poor judgment! And you honestly will consider keeping this unstable guy on your staff? The written word is powerful—especially in your line of work. What a disappointment to this reader if you choose to keep this man on as a writer."

Another: "Good morning Jim. I am a former councilman and Mayor Pro Tem from Keller [next to Watauga]. I am writing to ask you to reinstate Dave Lieber. He is a fine individual who has done many great things in this community. While I was serving on the city council and Dave had just start-ed working with the *Star-Telegram*, I actually tried to get him fired because of his coverage of politics at that time. I was wrong trying to do that. ... I firmly believe one is innocent until proven guilty. I see no reason to suspend him."

One more: "Don't suspend Dave Lieber. You should give him a bonus. He did what we all want to do to our smart-mouth kids."

A lawyer friend coached me on the legal language for my buyout agreement: "Both the *Star-Telegram* and Lieber agree that Lieber accepts the terms of this buyout voluntarily.

"The *Star-Telegram* further acknowledges that Lieber was, up to and including the day of his resignation, a model employee at the *Star-Telegram*, whose columns and community activities as a representative of the *Star-Telegram* helped create a positive view of the *Star-Telegram* within those communities."

If I didn't have that language included, the lawyer said, "you will be leaving under a cloud that will follow you for a very long time."

This was all so terribly sad to me. My dream of becoming a newspaper columnist was a 22-year journey. I was 14 when I chose my career path, and everything I did from then until the *Star-Telegram* hired me at age 36 was aimed at that goal.

After 15 years, being a columnist was everything I ever dreamed of. I didn't want to give it up. I knew that I probably would never be a newspaper columnist again. And I worried that Austin would take the blame for this happening. I didn't want that on his conscience.

I tried to keep up a brave front. Told my

family that I had many more opportunities. Actually, a receipt from one quick impulsive trip to the food market showed my true, fretful state of mind.

Fig Newtons $2.75
Hostess Suzy Q's $3
Oreos $2.50
7UP $3.88
Hershey's Syrup $1.50
Blue Bell Ice Cream $5.79

I had a problem, possibly, with the district attorney, too. My mother had died years before. But I could hear her: "You and your big mouth. You just had to do that, didn't you?"

Yes, I did.

In 2002, Tim Curry, the Tarrant County district attorney for more than 30 years, faced the election challenge of his career. His opponent was a former prosecutor in his office, a talented and brash woman with a career courtroom record of 96-4.

In an era when schools are closed because of fear of snipers, and hijacked airplanes are used to kill thousands, I want my prosecutors to be more pit bull than basset hound. I want my district attorney to be passionate and wild-eyed and make criminals quake in their stolen sneakers.

Tim Curry, the Tarrant County district attorney, is the basset hound that sits there speaking softly with sad eyes and a long face. He has had a great run of 30 years. I say it's time for his retirement dinner. Give him a gold watch and a standing ovation of gratitude. ...

When was the last time you saw him on TV? A top prosecutor doesn't have to be a hot dog in front of the cameras, but a little bit of crime-busters images wouldn't hurt to scare off the criminals.

"I do that by design," Curry told me. "I don't think my name ought to be in the paper or that I ought to be on television. I ought to be doing my job. I mean, she's got to run on something.

"We're squeaky clean here," he continued. "We've got a good record. We're probably the best district attorney's office in the state."

His opponent, Terri Moore, said, "I will be the top prosecutor who is in that courtroom. Not just on high-publicity cases to get my name in the paper. I will be leading those younger prosecutors by example. I will pat them on the back and tell them they do a good job and chew them out when they don't.

"Mr. Curry, when he comes to work in the mornings, he gets off the private elevator. I've seen it for 10 years. And he walks down the long hall. He never looks left. He never looks right. He goes straight down the hall to that office and nobody talks to him. It's not like he says, 'You did a good job in that case yesterday.'"

How did Curry respond?

"I take the elevator because there's where I park," he told me. "That's the only way to get into the building. It's also the elevator all the judges use."

Curry won re-election that year, and again four years later. I hoped Curry and his staff didn't remember those election columns. But how could they forget?

On a Watauga police report about my arrest, the district attorney's role was clear. A detective wrote: "After reviewing the case, it was forwarded to the Tarrant County District Attorney's Office for consultation. I later received an e-mail message from the assistant district attorney indicating the charges will be accepted upon filing."

Yes, Mom. Me and my big mouth. Whenever I thought about this, I went and ate Hostess Suzy Q's.

A couple of local writers skewered me. They saw things quite differently than I did.

Dan McGraw wrote in *Fort Worth Weekly's* blog:

> Parents are up in arms about how Lieber was treated. Postings online over this arrest have been numerous, with most parents writing about how they were treated by their parents. Walking home such a short distance was common place punishment back in the day, and certainly not anything police should have been involved in.
>
> My problem with Lieber and his employer is their reaction to this case. On Aug. 15th, two days after the incident, Lieber posted a column where he basically said he was a bad parent for punishing his kid in such a manner. The S-T then suspended him after the arrest until the case is resolved.

The lines in Lieber's apologetic column that get me riled are as follows:

"My thoughts are many. For one, back in the 1960s if my parents had told me to 'walk home by yourself' when I misbehaved, no one would have thought twice. But what flew years ago doesn't fly today. I could have exposed my son to grave danger. I do know that. But in the moment of anger I didn't think clearly."

If Lieber was going to be charged with anything, it should have been for abandoning his balls.

Whether Lieber was writing this teary column with thoughts that this might influence the legal system in his favor is not known. But maybe he should have asserted his rights as a parent instead. The "caring person" who called the police should have been blasted by Dave. The police have no business getting involved in parental decisions that are warranted and do not harm that child.

I've had experiences with my now college age daughter that became a little physical at times. When she was 15 or 16, she always had to be on the computer with her chat friends. The computer was in my bedroom, and I would ask her to get off around midnight so I could get some sleep. Several times she refused and told me to go crash on the couch. My reaction? Crawl under the desk and rip out the plugs, pick her up off the chair and throw her into her bedroom. Some might call this "child endangering." I call it asserting my rights as a parent. And teaching her a lesson about how to deal with other people.

Instead of suspending Lieber, the S-T should have backed him. They should have stood by their "watchdog" and issued a statement that they believe he did no wrong.

Both Lieber and his employers are weenies in this case. Get a grip folks, and get a spine. He didn't leave a toddler in a parked car in 100 degree heat, nor did he beat the crap out of him. He told an 11-year-old he had enough of his antics, and told him to walk home. That was the logical and appropriate message to send. Instead we get whiny apologies and the suspension.

D Magazine editor Tim Rogers shared his take on "FrontBurner," the blog of the city magazine of neighboring Dallas. He saw it the same way as his Fort Worth counterpart:

Okay, I just went insane. I'm sitting here at my desk, yelling at my computer. Because someone just sent me a link to the story about Star-Telegram columnist Dave Lieber getting arrested for child abandonment. I gotta tell you, Lieber has driven me nervous. I've got a full-blown case of the howling fantods about what this guy did—but not for ditching the kid. ...

I say bully on you, Dave Lieber. Good show. The kid had it coming. As a parent, you've got to let those jerks who live in your house know that you mean business. When you count to three, if they haven't done what needs doing by three, then there's a price to be paid. It's up to you whether that's a hand to the rump or a pulled plug on the Wii.

Just so in this case. Lieber asked his kid to get a grip. Repeatedly. And then he showed the kid that his bad behavior had made him an unsuitable driving companion. Walk home, junior. On the way, think about the apology you'll make when you walk through the front door.

Listen, my mother did exactly this same thing to me. I was 7 or 8. We were eating at a McDonald's (I think) on Ross Avenue—excuse me, Cesar Chavez Avenue. ... I was being a brat. Neither my mom nor I can recall exactly what form this brattiness took. But she finally said something to the effect of: "Get in the car right now, or I'm leaving without you." I didn't, and she did.

So I plopped down and started to wait. Because I knew she'd be back. At least I thought she'd come back. Mom will come back, right?

Oh, of course she came back. Time ticks slower for young people. Her trip around the block felt like 20 minutes to me. When she pulled up, I leaped into the car, showered her with angel kisses, and promised to be a good boy for the rest of my life— a promise I've kept. At least that's the way I'm going to tell the story, because her memory obviously isn't good enough to contradict my version of events.

So the idea that Lieber was arrested for this is nuts. If there are facts I'm unaware of—if he regularly beats his son, if he traffics in barnyard porn— then I deserve the right to change my stance. But from what we know right now, Lieber should have gotten a pat on the back from the cops. Good on ya, buddy. Next time, if you want to use my Taser, give me a ring.

But almost worse than the arrest is the column Lieber wrote about the incident. It was titled "How Parents Can Learn From Serious Mistakes." WHAT? NO!! Don't bend to the pressure, man! YOU'RE A HERO TO FATHERS EVERYWHERE!! You did the right thing. Don't get all wimpy on us and allow as how you could have exposed your kid to "grave danger." It was breakfast! Home was just a few blocks away!! AND THE KID WAS ACTING LIKE A JERK! Lieber went on in his column to contact a parenting center and ask for their advice on how to deal with a situation like this. Listen, buddy, I hope you only did that because you knew you'd eventually have to face a judge, and the column would be a swell way to show contrition. Because otherwise, yeah, the paper should take your column away.

After reading that, I went for the Blue Bell Ice Cream and Hershey's Syrup.

Here are some things about Austin and me that perhaps you should know: From the beginning, we were exceptionally close. His first couple of years were spent by my side. I called it a social experiment. It began when I searched my newspaper's archives for mentions of the phrase "working mother" and found 268. I checked for "working father" and found only 21. One story was headlined, "Fatherhood mostly remains a closet issue in the workplace." When Karen's 90-day maternity leave ended and she returned to her job, I decided to try life as a working dad. My plan was to care for Austin from 8 a.m. to 6 p.m. on weekdays and work on my columns during his naps, at night and whenever possible. Most days, he went where I went. But there were a lot of playground stops, too. When I wrote upstairs in my home office, he napped beside me. I took him to elementary schools where I explained my experiment to young audiences. We went to Rotary clubs, chamber of commerce events, even the regular Monday morning editorial board meeting at my newspaper, where I joked that he was the swing vote. Whenever there was a place I couldn't take him, such as a courtroom or a government meeting, I hired a sitter. For about 18 months, this

arrangement worked. And, honestly, it was the happiest and most rewarding experience of my life. Then he grew bigger, started walking and became active. We kept up our partnership as long as we could. But eventually, he began spending more time with other children under the care of a neighborhood mom who ran a small licensed child care center.

During this time, I began seeing every aspect of the world through my son's innocent eyes. Whenever I introduced him to something new, I was struck by the profoundness of learning everything from scratch, of experiencing new sights and sounds, of trying to figure it all out. I began to write columns about our discoveries to-

Austin at a 2000 George W. Bush rally in Dallas.

gether. The high school band on the practice field after school. ("The band! I want to see band. No see football.") A 2000 George W. Bush campaign rally. ("Daddy, why did George W. Bush wave at me?") His first baseball team. ("What transpired at that first practice," I wrote, "could possibly be described as the single most chaotic hour in the history of organized baseball.") And my favorite: our trip to a church that had constructed an outdoor labyrinth, a meditation path, that I used to introduce Austin to the idea of God. (Headline: "Search to find God, like circle, is never-ending.")

He was always happy to help me with my newspaper projects, whether it was visiting the modern art museum to see if he could color better than the million-dollar paintings on the wall, or, when he was 5, running for governor of Texas. It was a crazy idea, but it actually worked. We made buttons that showed a picture of him standing in front of the Alamo in a Texas flag shirt. The buttons read: Austin J. Lieber for Governor. We sold them for $5, earned a few thousand dollars and donated the money to Summer Santa, an all-volunteer children's charity I had co-founded the year Austin was born. The timing was right.

The two major party candidates for governor were locked in a mudslinging contest, calling each other money launderers and bribe-takers. I offered Austin as the candidate of maturity. His motto was: "Vote for Austin. He's clean. He takes a bath every night." Whenever anyone would mention it to Austin—and lots of adults did because they read about it in the newspaper—he'd smile and say bashfully, "That's just a joke my dad and I are doing."

When I offered a button to one of his "opponents," Gov. Rick Perry, he handed it back and turned away. When I asked Perry for a humorous comment for my column he replied, "Oh, no comment!" Nope, the governor didn't think it was funny. But Texas House Speaker Pete Laney liked the idea. I quoted the speaker in my column saying, "What I like about his candidacy is his first name because I have a grandson named Austin. Hopefully, he will be part of the generation that won't succumb to the negative politics that's going on now. A lot of it is consultant-driven. It's a lot easier for a paid consultant to say negative things than it is to say positive things. The neat thing about somebody like Austin is that in a campaign he would probably say what he thinks. The honesty of a young man like this is what we all want in politics."

On Election Day and afterward, dozens of fed-up voters told me they had actually voted for my son as a write-in protest vote. I called the elections office to find out how many votes he got. They said they didn't count them.

In his concession speech, printed in my column (he sometimes wrote in my place when I was "on vacation"), Austin urged the adults to end "these horrible and c h i l d i s h games of bad-

Two of Austin's column headshots used when he "wrote" my column. He's a natural.

mouthing their opponents. ... Grow up and do the right thing." He added, "This change will be forced on them like the vegetables that are forced upon me at dinnertime." He was such a good sport. I'll always be grateful to my son for the way he played along with my columnist pranks.

From all our time together, I knew him so well. I could anticipate his needs. Read his mind. See inside his soul. Mine was more of a motherly intuition than a fatherly one. What we had was special. I never felt so close to another human being. I really understood him. Because, really, he is so me.

Now when I see him as a teenager standing at the kitchen counter eating a peanut butter and jelly sandwich at 11 p.m., I truly see myself. The good and the not so good. He has the same lack of patience, the same belligerence. There must be a belligerent gene that is passed down. I have it; he does, too. I remember the first time I saw it in him. It was after dinner. He was 13 months old. For some reason, he got angry and began wailing. He wouldn't stop. There wasn't any apparent reason for it. He just stayed angry. I tried to quiet him down. I took him outside in the dark and walked him up and down our street. I hugged him, tried to console him. Made up a rhythmic song ... "Boom, choca-latta, boom, boom, ssss. Boom, choca-latta, boom, boom, sss." He wouldn't calm down. He was defiant. I feared at that moment that my late mother's great prophesy from 40 years ago ("*God is going to punish you when you have children*") was going to come true. I was going to raise a son like me.

Dave's mom

When I began to act out as a young boy in the early 1960s, there wasn't a name for it. Now it's called oppositional defiant disorder. Early images that stick in my memory: The first-grade teacher whose class I was transferred to mid-year suddenly became ill and left for the day when I was placed in her class. (My mother overheard her complaining that she got stuck with the worst kid in the first grade.) I remember the intermediate school principal who suspended me for a week after I cursed him out for no reason. I remember the "Green Wall" in eighth grade. ("Mr. Lieber, go face the Green Wall.") And I'd press my nose against the wall in the main corridor. When the bell rang and classes let out, I was like the guy locked in the stockade for all to gawk at in the town square.

Me at 11 years old.

Oppositional defiant disorder is defined as a pattern of disobedient, hostile and defiant behavior toward authority figures, according to Google Health. "More common in boys than girls. Some studies have shown it affects 20 percent of school-age children. However, most experts believe this figure is high due to changing definitions of normal childhood behavior, and possible racial, cultural and gender biases. This behavior typically starts at age 8. The cause of this disorder is unknown, and may be due to a combination of biology and parenting or environmental factors." Symptoms include not following adults' requests, anger and resentment toward others, blaming others for one's mistakes, constant troubles at school and an easy loss of temper. "In many cases, children with oppositional defiant disorder grow up to have conduct disorder as adults. ... Be consistent about rules and fair consequences at home. Don't make punishments too harsh or inconsistent. Model the right behaviors for your child. Abuse and neglect increases the chances that this condition will occur."

My parents neither abused nor neglected me. They were befuddled more than anything else about what to do. Nobody knew. But Mom put her own curse of revenge on me.

That belligerent gene. Passed on to Austin. Along with my own behaviors and impulses. There's no denying that our attributes are similar. You can see it in a side-by-side comparison of our school report cards, 40 years apart.

"David's constant talking and calling out is not considerate of the rights of the other children because he distracts them from their work. David must control his temper and learn to settle differences amicably."

"Austin needs to focus on proper classroom participation instead of side conversations, arguments and unwanted comments. This often results in him disrupting his classmates, and this also interferes with his own learning. He always seems

to want to talk to his neighbors and disturb them. We have talked about his need to exercise more self-control."

"David does not concentrate on his work as he is anxious to finish first. Therefore, his work isn't always neat and he makes mistakes that he could have avoided."

"Austin needs to spend more time revising and redrafting writing to ensure that it makes sense. He must check final drafts for misspelling and other errors."

"David must learn to act properly on the bus. He is very restless at times. I should like to talk to you about this."

"Austin is a gifted boy, I am sure he could do a better job if he used his time more efficiently."

All of Austin's troubles in school, however, were minor, especially when compared to mine. Oh boy. Mine were doozies. When I did something stupid, it wasn't merely seen in some school classroom. The result wasn't usually a simple hour of detention after school, as it is in Austin's world. No, when I fell, I fell hard. In public. On the world's big stage. Literally. Like the incident at McDonald's.

Doozy #1. 1969. I am 12 years old. I sing in the Metropolitan Opera's children's chorus as an after-school job. Lincoln Center is in my neighborhood, two subway stops from my family's apartment on the Upper West Side of Manhattan. I am paid $3 for every opera performance I am in; $1 for each rehearsal. I do this for three years, earning between $200 and $400 each year. I sing in Italian in *La Gioconda*. I sing in French in *Carmen*. I sing in English in *Hansel and Gretel*. I never really understand what I am singing in these operas. None of the kids in the chorus does. That's not important. What's important is that we know the words, can sing well enough and remember what we are supposed to do on stage. I've never taken voice lessons and cannot read a note of music. But that doesn't matter. My fifth-grade teacher recommended me for a tryout. I sang *My Country, Tis of Thee* to the mae-

This photo of the Metropolitan Opera's children's chorus appeared in a 1967 issue of Opera News when I was 10. I'm front and center in my gingerbread-boy costume for Hansel and Gretel.

stro. That was it. I'm in. My pals and I in the chorus have so much fun hanging out backstage at the legendary opera house. We play on the expensive sets. Stare at the big-ego performers who stop rehearsals and rant for reasons we can't understand. We have our run of the place, prancing around in our opera costumes as little soldiers (*Carmen*), peasant children (*La Giaconda*) and gingerbread kids (*Hansel and Gretel*). In *Hansel*, during the final scene, we stand on stage as captive cookies under the spell of the Wicked Witch. In one of the best known acts of oppositional defiant disorder, Hansel and Gretel push the witch in the oven. Then they touch our noses and break the evil spell. We emerge from our gingerbread trance and become real boys and girls again. Joyously, we sing: "We are safe. We are free. Our thanks to you." Then we open the oven and grab the remains of the witch, now a Styrofoam cutout of the original witch singer, painted brown with a scorched frown on its face. We in the children's chorus are allowed to rip the Styrofoam into pieces and celebrate the witch's demise. Here's the best part. Whoever captures the head is allowed to take this trophy home in addition to the $3. I yearn for that witch's head the way a hunter wants a wall mount with antlers. Every boy in the chorus wants that head.

One Saturday matinee performance, broadcast live on the Texaco Metropolitan Opera International Radio Network, we pull the Styrofoam cutout out of the oven. For the first time, I grab the witch's head. I can't believe it! This is my moment. But another boy singer, Kris, he grabs it, too. And darn him, he won't let go. Neither will I.

In a second, our battle becomes a tug of war on center stage. Then one of us—I can't remember who —throws the first punch. There's no hesitation. The fight is on. On live international radio, on the main stage of the greatest opera house in the world, we are going at it. The witch head breaks into pieces. The opera ends. We walk off the stage to stone-cold looks from adults in the wings. A day later, I get a phone call. I am fired as a gingerbread boy.

Doozy #2. 1971. I am 14. I host a television show on the NBC television network that's shown live on Saturday mornings across the United States. (Yes, growing up in Manhattan offers kids great opportunities.) The show is called *Take a Giant Step*. It's an hour long and unscripted. Each Saturday three teenagers talk about issues that are important to kids. The idea is to give America's youth an alternative to Saturday morning cartoons. My eighth-grade English teacher recommended me for this. I am one of about 30 kids in the pool of hosts. I get to host four shows during the TV season. A million kids across the country watch. It's a great experiment in children's programming. Real kids. Talking like you. But actually, it's boring to watch. We aren't trained, so we talk over one another a lot. We say "um" and "you know" way too much. It's a bit painful to watch. But after every show, I walk down Broadway, near where I live in Manhattan, and adults recognize me. I even get a few fan letters, one from Pam, a girl in Nebraska who fictionalizes me as "cute, tall Dave."
However.
There is a producer who butts heads with me. Or rather, I butt heads with her. It's *her* show. She's a strong Italian-American woman who wants to control everything. (I am too young to realize that this

is a producer's job.) And this woman, well, she is on to me. She is so on to me that she won't cut me a break. At least I don't think so. She is producing a show about the future. I am one of her three teen hosts for that topic. A week before the show, we are supposed to fly to Florida to visit "the house of the future" so we can talk about it on the TV show. Before the trip, the producer takes me aside and warns me to behave. She says that she can't go, but she is putting her assistant in personal charge of me. I am not to act up or get out of line. Do I understand?

The 1971 NBC publicity photo for my TV show about the future. With me are my co-hosts, Rhodina Williams and Tom White. I was 14.

I am surly. She is picking on me. I grumpily tell her not to worry. Leave me alone. I didn't do anything wrong. Not yet.

She is right about me. At the airport where we are to fly to Fort Lauderdale, I see a sign at the check-in counter that warns not to carry explosives on board. I say quietly to one of my teen co-hosts, "Better not have a bomb in your purse." The airline employee at the desk looks up.

"What did you say?"

"Nothing."

"No, what did you say? I heard what you said."

Some men come and take me into a small room. I say over and over, "I was just joking." They won't let me on the flight. The others go without me. The assistant who is assigned to watch me is so angry she can't even speak to me. We catch a later flight on a different airline. I arrive in Florida around nightfall. Most of the day is over. Everyone there is embarrassed for me, but nobody is more ashamed than I am.

A day later, back at NBC offices at 30 Rockefeller Plaza, upstairs in the *Take a Giant Step* offices, the producer waits for me. She is angrier, more on fire than anyone at school, at home or even at the Metropolitan Opera. She gives me such a tongue-lashing that I start to cry. Once I start, I can't stop. But she doesn't stop. I run out into the hallway so I can cry in the men's room.

Before our show goes live on national television, she takes me aside and says, "Someday, David, you will understand."

The assistant who was stuck with me at the airport becomes a vice president at the ABC television network. This is how a TV career ends at age 14.

My legal dilemma was hot talk around town. Callers to local radio stations debated my parenting skills and the conduct of the Watauga police. Many came to my defense; a few did not. The *Austin American-Statesman* published a story by Chuck Lindell ("Father's arrest ignites debate over child abandonment") that asked experts in the Texas state capital how they viewed my case.

> Much of the debate surrounding Lieber's arrest focuses on whether leaving an 11-year-old in a restaurant parking lot was unreasonably risky and whether police overreacted. ...

> Dayna Blazey, a Travis County assistant district attorney, cannot recall a similar charge of child abandonment in her 13 years on the Child Protection Team, a collection of law enforcement agencies and other organizations that investigate child abuse allegations.

"Do I think that this happens? Yeah," Blazey said. "Is it something law enforcement gets involved with frequently and it leads to a criminal investigation? It's not something I see."

Most of Travis County's abandonment cases involve children left in hot cars and kids left in stores by parents who shoplift and run to avoid capture, she said.

Still, Blazey cautioned, it's difficult to judge whether the Watauga police overreacted.

"We don't have all the facts," she said. "In looking at these cases, we look at previous history. They may have information about prior instances involving these two people."

Eric Franklin, an investigations supervisor for Child Protective Services in Austin, said his investigations of similar incidents over 5 1/2 years have focused on three things:

Was the child safe based on his age, maturity and ability to reason?

Were the circumstances dangerous? Was it late at night, or in gang territory, or too far from home to walk?

What were the father's intentions? Did he return quickly?...

"He might have been trying to teach his son a lesson, maybe scare him. I don't know if that is way out of bounds," Franklin said. "Would I do it? Probably not. ... I wouldn't want to put my daughter in that situation. It's a bad world out there."

Parenting is a difficult and demanding task, said Kelli Williamson, clinical director for the Austin Child Guidance Center, a nonprofit that provides therapy for children and their families. But leaving a child behind raises issues about safety and effective parenting, she said.

"Abandoning your child is not going to teach them appropriate behavior. It also can teach them that if they do something wrong, then they're going to be left," she said. "You want to work through the conflict and come up with reasonable consequences, not deal with it by walking away."

I understood that what everyone else in the world thought about my case was not important. This was now a legal matter. Heading to a criminal grand jury. Witnesses, evidence and testimony would be presented. That's how my future would be decided. On this front, I believed I had problems.

There were four witnesses cited in the police report. Some of them stated that they saw things that I know didn't happen. Enough of their comments were exaggerations, even falsehoods, that taken together, they could create the impression of a situation that was meaner and more dangerous than it actually was.

The police report summary states that witnesses "observed the adult male and Austin Lieber inside the restaurant arguing and the adult male scolded and cursed at the boy, making him stand against the wall."

No, I asked him to sit at another table. (After my Green Wall experience in eighth grade, I never asked any of my children to face a wall.) I didn't curse at him either.

Several witnesses said they saw Austin grab the door handle as I backed the car out of its parking spot. True. One witness wrote in his statement, "The man continued to back up with the child bumping into the car."

Austin didn't bump into the car. He stepped back when he couldn't open the door. He had no bruises or injuries. If he had, police most likely would have noted it.

This was going to be my word against theirs.

The most notorious story about the Watauga police department didn't come from one of my "tickets." *Star-Telegram* police reporter Leila Fadel reported in 2005 that a Watauga woman dialed 911 for what some later believed was a flimsy reason. She said she couldn't stop her daughters from fighting. Her 12-year-old had kicked a hole in a door.

The Watauga dispatcher responded, "OK. Do you want us to come over to shoot her?"

The woman was silent for several seconds, according to a tape of the call.

"Are you there?" the dispatcher asked.

"Excuse me?" the woman said.

The dispatcher said he was joking and quickly apologized. After the call, he told his supervisor what happened. "I would take it back if I could, but I can't," he said. "I'm just very sorry that I did it. It was a poor choice of things to say."

The incident gained national attention. The dispatcher was reprimanded by the police chief. The chief said a reprimand was suitable punishment because the dispatcher quickly confessed his error.

The mother responded, "I do not have words to tell you how shocked I am that someone is allowed to do this. You don't do people like this, and then get a slap on the wrist."

Many questioned the mother's parenting skills and wondered if she abused the 911 system. Her home was staked out by TV news reporters. Her neighbors were asked about her fitness to be a parent.

The dispatcher, meanwhile, was hailed as a hero. He appeared on Fox News. A talk radio host beat the drums on the dispatcher's behalf, then rewarded him with a trip to Disney World.

In my newspaper, columnist colleague Bud Kennedy wrote, "Watauga is the latest setting where talk shows have turned a complex news story into a dumbed-down, 10-minute morality play. ... The problem was not that the mother called 911. Mental-health professionals said parents of children with emotional problems should always call 911 when disturbances turn physically threatening. The problem was that the Watauga call taker took the mother lightly."

No, that story wasn't one of mine. I was busy writing my own tickets.

Ticket #12 — Police Make Lewd Comments to Young Woman

A school crossing guard arrives at a school zone for her afternoon shift, but she tells her daughter to stay in the car. A Watauga police sergeant asks about the daughter. The mother answers that the daughter, 18, is not allowed to step out because she is wearing clothing that is inappropriate. The teen's skirt is too short, and her blouse is too revealing. I write:

As the guard helped children cross the street, she watched angrily as the sergeant walked to her car and asked her daughter to step out. The mother chastised the sergeant, but the sergeant told her to go away because he was in charge.

The sergeant flirted with the daughter, the mother said, talking with her about her clothing and other matters, much to the discomfort of the mother.

The woman also said the sergeant discussed whether her daughter wore underwear, and she said that he used foul language, even after she asked him to stop.

My story continues with the arrival of a police lieutenant who makes a joke about applying for a job as the girl's boyfriend. The mother complains to the department. There's an internal investigation. The sergeant is forced to resign. The lieutenant is suspended for five days without pay and placed on six months' probation.

"Unprofessional conduct by a few bad seeds has reflected poorly on the many good officers who do good work," I write in the paper. "This has to stop."

00013

CITATION AND COMPLAINT

Ticket #13 — City Employees Fail to Call Police When 5-Year-Old Boy Is Sexually Abused

Two city employees were suspended and a third reprimanded after employees did not properly respond when a 5-year-old boy reported that he was sexually assaulted outside the Watauga Recreation Center.

This is a deficiency of the worst kind. A city absolutely must protect the children who come to its recreation center, even, as in this case, children who come to play outside the center. When a crime of this nature occurs, reaction must be swift and strong.

In this case, the staff did not react professionally. Supervisors were not notified in a timely manner, and when they were, they did not immediately call police, as they should have done.

00014

CITATION AND COMPLAINT

Ticket #14 —Officer Who Criticizes Department Forced to Resign

A new police chief, a former Army officer, calls the entire department together for an introductory meeting at the Watauga Public Library.

"Chief, are we free to talk?" asks Officer Ted Gerardi, the department's K-9 officer.

"Yes, you are."

"Then forgive me if I'm blunt. It's well known and should be well known to you at this time that your immediate command staff is comprised of a pack of liars and thieves. And we would like to know if you have any plans on dealing with this and, if so, when."

Forty uniformed officers watch as the chief calmly replies, "You and I can discuss this in my office."

Two weeks later, Gerardi is called to the chief's office. But he isn't asked to explain his remarks. Instead, he is asked to explain why he lied on his police application form 22 years before.

The outside auditor who criticized the department (Ticket #8) recommended that all department members undergo a background check. Gerardi's check showed that he had been arrested three times in his youth and convicted on a theft charge. Yet on his application to the department in 1982, he had answered that he had never been arrested.

The K-9 officer's explanation for this would lead to the end of his career in Watauga.

> Gerardi recalls talking to a captain, Bill Keating, who later became Watauga city manager. He said he told Keating that he had been arrested three times.
>
> As Gerardi remembers, Keating told him, "I ain't worried about no chicken thieves. I don't want any bank robbers working for me." Keating, he said, told him to answer no to the question because arrests didn't show up on background checks, including one before Gerardi was hired. They assumed that his record had been purged.
>
> Keating, now sheriff-elect for Montague County, said last week: "I really don't recall that happening. If it happened, it happened, and if it didn't, it didn't."

The new police chief says he is disturbed by Gerardi's explanation. He gives the K-9 officer a choice: resign or be fired. He says Gerardi's previous comments about "liars and thieves" have nothing to do with his leaving. (The chief never follows up on these comments to find out what Gerardi means.) The chief says, "The thing that pushed me over the edge was when he said, 'It's not my fault. Keating made me do it.'" (The chief is new in town, and doesn't yet understand the Watauga way.)

Gerardi loses his job. Keating, who has gone from cafe owner to county sheriff, hires him as Montague County's new K-9 officer.

Gerardi sues the city of Watauga, which leads to the next ticket I write.

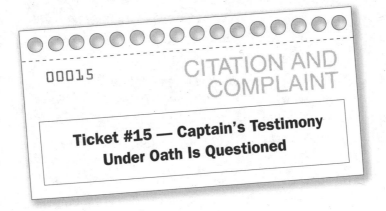

00015   CITATION AND COMPLAINT

Ticket #15 — Captain's Testimony Under Oath Is Questioned

Gerardi's lawyer hopes to prove that in the Watauga police department, all punishments are not equal. Captain Bill Crawford, who as an investigator, was charged with "substandard work" by a police detective in an indecent exposure case

(Ticket #5), testifies under oath in the lawsuit.

The lawyer asks Crawford in a deposition about his previous order to backdate the air-pack safety logs (Ticket #9). Crawford testifies that the re-created logs matched original safety checks that were not properly recorded.

Crawford first asked firefighter Steve Caudle to do it. Caudle refused. Caudle's testimony about what happens differs from his boss Crawford's. I report what happens, starting with Caudle's testimony:

> "I said, 'You're wanting me to fill in these blanks knowing that I'm not the one who checked these air packs several days back, and you're wanting me to put my name on there?' And he [Crawford] said, 'Yeah, go ahead. It ain't no big deal.'"
>
> Caudle testified that he took the logs out of the office and complained to several co-workers. He testified that he "couldn't believe it, what he was wanting me to do, and I didn't do it."
>
> "Did you feel like that was dishonest?" the lawyer asked.
>
> "That's why I didn't do it, yes, sir," Caudle replied. …
>
> But under oath in his deposition, Crawford was asked: "So if Mr. Caudle says that you asked him to go back and create records that did not previously exist, you would deny that?"
>
> "Yes," Crawford answered.
>
> "Do you think Mr. Caudle is a liar?" the lawyer asked.
>
> "Yes, if he says that," Crawford answered. …

When Jeffrey Hawkins, the firefighter whom Crawford convinced to change the logs, gave his deposition, he was asked about making the changes. He answered by invoking the Fifth Amendment 11 times.

00016

CITATION AND COMPLAINT

Ticket #16 — Detective Botches ID Theft Case

Watauga police arrest a man suspected of identity theft. He carries in his bag six cell phones, torn bank records that do not belong to him and other papers that list names, dates of birth, Social Security numbers, bank account numbers and balances, credit card balances and personal checks, all belonging to other people.

A Watauga detective assigned to the case tries to find ID theft victims so charges can be filed, but the detective says he can't find anyone.

Five months pass. Then, in a nearby town, the same man is arrested again by a different police department. In a bag in the man's car, police find a credit card machine, hotel receipts for other people, and a binder that contains personal infor-mation of 150 people, including their names, birth-dates, Social Security numbers and photocopies of their driver's licenses. This time, the second police department presses charges.

I decide to test the Watauga detective's work. I wonder if I can find the victims that he says he couldn't find. It takes me less than an hour.

In a matter of minutes, Star-Telegram *news researchers Marcia Melton and Cathy Belcher used Internet search engines to find a local phone number for a man whom the detective reported he could not find. I called the man at his home, left a message, and within an hour he called back.*

I told him that his name had shown up in a Watauga police report and that the detective said he couldn't find him.

The man explained that he was on medical leave last year and was usually at home. If the detective had written him a letter, visited his home or called him, the man said, he would have responded.

"This is the first I have heard of this," the man told me. "I'm relieved that you got hold of me and told me."

He said he was frustrated by the detective's lack of follow-up.

"I'm disappointed that I wasn't contacted," he said. "The police department should have various avenues to find me. If you can find me, they can find me."

CITATION AND
COMPLAINT

00017

Ticket #17 — Police Chief
Candidate Has Resume Problem

Watauga authorities announce they have found the man they want to hire as the next police chief. A day later, I raise questions about the prospect's educational background. The candidate says he has a master's degree in police administration from St. John's University. St. John's University in New York City is one of the largest Catholic universities in the United States. But I learn his degree is from St. John's University in Louisiana. It's an unaccredited university, a diploma mill. A state official who monitors accredited and unaccredited schools says the future police chief is "someone who doesn't know enough to see a fraudulent or substandard education when he sees one."

The job candidate tells me in an interview that he told city officials about his education. "I didn't try to hide anything," he says. "They all know." But when I ask those same city officials if they knew, they say they did not. "You hit me in the face here," says the city manager, Kerry Lacy, who made the selection. "This blows me away."

An hour after my interview with the job candidate, he sends an e-mail message to Watauga City Hall: "Due to the recent controversy over my educational background, I respectfully withdraw my name from the hiring process."

Lacy, who made the pick from 58 candidates, says, "So I'm back to the drawing board."

While interviewing Lacy, we talk about how to do background checks on candidates. The city manger acknowledges that hiring a police chief is one of the toughest parts of his job (he's gone through three at this point). Then he asks me to help him do background checks on the next batch of candidates. I tell him that's probably not a good idea.

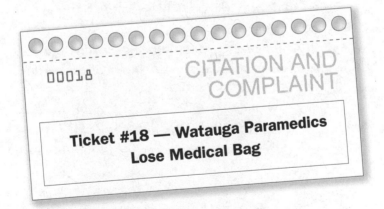

CITATION AND COMPLAINT

00018

Ticket #18 — Watauga Paramedics Lose Medical Bag

Three Watauga paramedics are called to a house to treat an elderly woman's leg. They transport her to the hospital. Later, the paramedics realize they left one of their medical bags at her house. A paramedic calls and leaves a message about the bag. But there's no follow-up to retrieve it.

The next day, Watauga police are called back to the house. A man who is the woman's grandson has died of an apparent drug overdose while his grandmother is in the hospital. Investigators find the contents of the lost Watauga medical bag strewn about the house. There are unopened syringes and other items spread everywhere. But there are no narcotics in the bag. The only item that appears to have been opened is a bottle of nitroglycerine, which is used to treat victims of heart attacks because it helps open arteries.

No serious attempt was made to retrieve the medical bag.

Paramedics never reported the bag missing to their supervisor until after the body was found.

The paramedics' supervisor, Capt. Bill Crawford, did not discipline the three paramedics involved. There were no administrative hearings or suspensions, records show.

Only afterward did Watauga begin recording the contents of its medical bags. Although Crawford insisted that nothing was missing, there were no records to verify the claim. ...

Lacy, the city manager, said: "I'm very upset, very disturbed, very concerned about the professionalism of the department as a whole. ... We will become a professional organization."

A follow-up investigation shows the man did not die from anything he found in the medical bag. He died from an accidental overdose of prescription drugs. Eventually, the three paramedics are suspended for one 24-hour shift each.

Two years after this happens, I am arrested by Watauga police. Because of a potential conflict of interest, I haven't written about the city in the newspaper since.

For 10 years, on the second Saturday of every May, I organized a fundraiser in what I called "beautiful downtown Watauga" for the children's charity I co-founded in 1997. The charity, Summer Santa (www.SummerSanta.org), serves 21 cities, six school districts and a dozen area charities in North Texas. We send several hundred children in need to summer camps each year, distribute several thousand toys each summer, and provide free medical checkups, and back-to-school clothing, school supplies and other after-school activities. In our first dozen years, Summer Santa served 30,000 children. The best part is Summer Santa is all-volunteer with no physical office or overhead. The corps of mom volunteers I work with each year spends what we raise on the children's programs we created. It's a passion of mine, and a way to stay true to the *Fort Worth Star-Telegram's* century-old tradition of helping our North Texas communities. (Our founder, Amon G. Carter Sr., said famously, "You can't live off your community. You must live with it.")

My event in Watauga served as the charity's main fundraiser. The Yankee Cowboy Celebrity Miniature Golf & Bowling Tournament was a fun, satirical takeoff on real celebrity golf events. I, of course, was the Yankee Cowboy. We held it at Brunswick Watauga Lanes, less than a mile from City Hall. There was a miniature golf course outside the bowling alley. Once a year, we filled them both. The money raised, averaging $20,000 a year, went to Summer Santa's summer camp fund.

We attracted about 200 participants. I organized contests among the mayors of all the nearby towns and also contests among schools, churches and other groups. After Sept. 11, 2001, as a way to honor police and firefighters, I created an annual contest featuring local police and fire departments, too. Usually, about a dozen teams representing area cities came to play. After they played, we fed the police and firefighters and their families. Then they could spend the rest of the day bowling as guests of the bowling lanes.

Watauga was my host city, and Watauga's mayor, whoever was in office during those 10 years, always played in my tournament. (One year a Watauga mayor won the mayor's trophy. But the other mayors told me later that his buddies helped his ball along.) The city seemed proud to host my little tournament. By proclamation, the City Council officially recognized tournament day as "Summer Santa Day in Watauga."

But after all those "tickets" I wrote, Watauga police and firefighters stopped attending. That was understandable. However, my goal was to bring everyone together to celebrate the Summer Santa idea—helping kids year-round, not just at the end-of-the-year holidays. (Over the years, the charity has assisted hundreds of Watauga kids.) So I asked City Manager Lacy if he could get the firefighters and police to come back and play. He promised that he would, and he kept his word.

Me (center) as the Yankee Cowboy at the annual miniature golf tournament for my charity.

The next tournament, the Watauga teams returned to play. I made a point of welcoming each member personally with a handshake. Even Capt. Crawford was there. He didn't seem happy about it.

That year, one of our volunteers slipped on the miniature golf course. She fell backward and hurt her knee. While she lay there, I called 911 and asked a Watauga dispatcher to send paramedics. Ten minutes later, after the ambulance arrived, paramedics worked to comfort the volunteer. When they were done, they got back into their ambulance. But as they began driving away, I saw that they left something on the ground.

A Watauga medical bag.

I grabbed the bag and trotted after the ambulance.

"Here, I know you didn't mean to leave this."

The paramedics thanked me. They looked embarrassed. I couldn't believe it. Of all the places. But I never wrote about it in the newspaper. The day, as I say, was about helping the Summer Santa kids.

From the moment I became a columnist, my soft spot was always helping kids. I wrote about kids who performed good deeds, kids who engaged in unusual school work, kids who helped other kids do better. My columns sought to promote a positive image of youth and help them excel. I believe that if you raise the bar higher for kids, they will exceed your expectations. My volunteer work on behalf of the student newspaper at my son's school was proof of that. I taught the children, grades two through 12, how to be newspapermen and women. Their work on the school paper won more than 100 state and national awards. We published a book of their best stories that won a national book award for education. In addition to that, my work for Summer Santa earned me the Will Rogers Humanitarian Award from the National Society of Newspaper Columnists. The award goes to a columnist who does positive works for his or her community.

Now, though, I stood accused of child abandonment and endangerment. The opposite of everything I had worked for.

In the days after my arrest, as searches on Google for my name spiked and the word "arrested" became closely associated with my persona, I felt helpless. I was in a dark place. But my emphasis was on keeping a positive frame of mind, especially as I tried to comfort my family. The curious part of me, though, wanted to understand why this was happening. What was I supposed to learn from it? Clearly, I understood and believed strongly that my first priority in every way must be my relationship with Austin. But beyond that?

Then I had an epiphany: I began to understand that I was performing an unexpected act of penance: *Dave Lieber is getting a dose of his own medicine.*

For 30 years I had done to others what now was being done to me. Something that happens in a moment becomes a newspaper story for days. Like a boulder rolling down a mountain, once it starts, it cannot be stopped.

Like many of those people I had written about, I was now frustrated about how I was being portrayed. Until this, I didn't understand how it felt.

It felt like this: Everything was out of control.

A penance.

Perhaps I, too, as Bud Kennedy had written, am a master at turning "a complex news story into a dumbed-down, 10-minute morality play." People I interview always caution me in cliches: *Get the other side of the story. Dig a little deeper to find out what's really going on here.* Certainly, they are not cliches to them.

In thousands of stories, I had exposed government, business and personal wrongdoing. I had also caused people severe hardships. Starting in college with that campus spying story, people sometimes lost their jobs because of what I wrote in the newspaper. Families were hurt and embarrassed. Now it was happening to me.

A penance.

Most disappointing was this: Through it all, of the dozens of people who wrote about my incident, not one reporter or blogger asked what seemed to be an easy and obvious question about an investigative columnist arrested by a police department. Even though several web comments posed the question, nobody followed up. And because I wasn't allowed to talk, the question never led to an answer. But I hope that if I am ever, as a reporter, covering a story such as this, I would remember to ask:

Did this guy ever write anything about that police department?

The phone rang. It was my lawyer checking in. Moore said he was talking to prosecutors about my case. He said he found five or six cases where abandonment means leaving a child in a field with the intent to abandon, or leaving a child on a bus for many hours. "Pretty drastic situations," he said. "This is not one of those."

He reminded me not to talk to anyone. I told him reporters were calling. He said I should refer them to him. But he wouldn't comment, either. "Don't stir the pot," he said. Moore is rare, a lawyer who doesn't clamor to get his face on the TV news. He hoped he would know something in a few days. I reminded him about my self-imposed deadline to resign from the paper and take a buyout if I faced a drawn-out legal battle. The deadline was less than a week away.

A few days later, on the last Friday in August 2008, Moore called again. He said he had good news. The prosecutors had decided to drop the charges. The case would go no further. I was sitting on the floor, taking notes. I dropped the pen and wrote nothing. Like that. Over. I thanked Moore for helping me. Told him I admired how he had kept to himself on my case. Told him I was grateful for his methods.

Karen was watching. When I hung up, I shouted the news. She cheered, feeling relief for the first time in days. My career was saved—days from that deadline to take a voluntary buyout. I found Austin and told him the news. A burden had been lifted from him, too. I called my boss at the paper and told her the news. Within an hour, the Star-Telegram confirmed the news and reported it on its website.

NO CHARGES TO BE FILED
AGAINST S-T COLUMNIST

In the story, a prosecutor said, "Once we got the information from the Watauga Police Department and reviewed it all, we determined that the elements did not rise to a felony offense."

Jim Witt, executive editor at my paper, commented: "We're gratified that the situation was quickly resolved and Dave will resume writing The Watchdog column immediately."

A headline on the *Austin American-Statesman* website announced: "Charges dropped against drive-off dad." And on another: "The Watchdog got watched — and fessed up to his mistake." Many people commented online and also in personal notes to me.

L.O.: We've all been parents and we've all done things "without thinking them through." Have a nice talk with your kid, become friends again, and move onward. Lay the past behind. Kids just need to know you love them unconditionally. (It is sort of like the same love a dog gives a person.)

the cynic: I thought the whole thing was over-wrought, too, until I hear the 911 calls. The kid may have been acting out, but Lieber was over the top. Apparently he threw a bigger fit than the kid. When the kid followed him out to the parking lot, witnesses say that Lieber nearly backed over him. Dad did not simply leave him at the restaurant.

jrp: Glad to hear common sense prevailed. And this whole "nearly backed over him" crap is just that. Take a second and think about it. Dad's in car backing out of parking spot. Kid is starting to realize dad is actually calling his bluff. Kid starts running toward car as car is moving backward at a whopping 4-5 mph and kid touches car/car touches kid. And these witnesses/numbskulls tell the cops and anyone within earshot that "HE ALMOST RAN OVER THE POOR BOY."

Rick E: Bad things may not have happened to the boy, but when you are sitting in a public restaurant witnessing a public spectacle such as it was, you hope that the parent would act like the PARENT and do whatever was necessary to control their child. Instead I witnessed 2 immature people

(1 young and 1 much older) arguing and displaying uncontrolled tempers. I saw a grown man jump up and stomp out of a restaurant and get into his small white SUV while a confused (child..boy..brat.. you choose) ran to catch up while his father blindly backed up and sped away with his son pulling frantically on a locked door running with the car as long as he could. The boy, left standing in the middle of a busy parking lot in the "drive thru" exit lane, was quickly moved to a safer location by CARING people who preferred to leave their warm meals to aid an abandoned kid instead of sitting still, eating their meals, indifferent to what was going on on the other side of the glass. We stood for over 15 minutes waiting for a grownup who had his "buttons" pushed by a small 11 yr old boy to return for his son. Some of you commend Leiber for admitting fault in his column. ... I see a person in the public's eye writing an essay on DAMAGE CONTROL who undoubtably knew this would make local headlines. I don't agree with this affecting his financial livelihood. I do however hope that he learns (soon) how to effectively lead his household and gain the respect of his son before the window of opportunity closes and his son has to learn the hard way that authority will be respected one way or another.

seanymph: Because someone had to stick their nose into it, this man's reputation has been tarnished and it costs him a lot of money. While I understand people wanting to protect children, they really need to not interfere unless they know exactly what's going on.

hb: Nice to hear the watchdog won't have to spend any time in the kennel.

april: Why is it a white man with money gets charges dropped, when if it was a white man with no money or even an African-American, they would have never dropped the charges? I just don't understand how some people can get away with stuff like that and others don't. It should be the same for everyone, not just people who have influences in the community.

Native Austinite: Thank goodness common sense prevailed. Oh, and April, you need to get that chip off your shoulder.

Colonel: I am so dismayed at the knee jerk reaction that started this unfortunate chain of events to unfold the way it did, and I cannot fathom how something so innocent and without any malice whatsoever could evolve into the firestorm that it has. And it sends out all sorts of warning bells that we live in a day and age where people are so quick to hit the panic button and jump to the wrong conclusions, without having all the facts in hand. It has really sobered me greatly to think that something like this could even happen in our society.

Annie: I have been reading your column for a while now and your column on your mistake was the best yet. Not owning up to your "mistake," but making me as a parent who goes through the same with my child feel like I was not alone. I cheer you for calling up the Parenting Center. I did the same just recently. I even signed up for a few classes coming up in the next few weeks as well. My son is also 11 and we have had quite a few defiant moments lately. I encourage you to write more on the subject when such things arise. I look forward to escaping in your columns and now I feel as I can really relate to you as well. I was going to leave my son at a nearby neighborhood market because of some stupid argument about doing homework when we arrived home. I know you are a busy person, so I will leave you alone. I just wanted to express my feelings about your public situation that quite a few of us struggle with privately time to time. Keep up the good work.

Rob: I'm glad that no charges were filed and you're back on the job. I read your column and you have helped a lot of people who had no one else to turn to. You made a mistake, you admitted it, you apologized. Apology accepted—get back to work.

That Friday afternoon, my boss called. "Do you have a column that we can run Sunday? I'd like to get it in the paper." I had one ready.

The next day, Saturday, a brief news story ran about the district attorney's decision to clear me. On the op-ed page, in a regular feature called "Cheers & Jeers," a reader commented: "Cheers: To the *Star-*

Telegram's Dave Lieber. After trying unsuccessfully for two months to get a water main leak repaired in Azle, I mailed a note to The Watchdog. A crew of six showed up in less than 36 hours and fixed the leak in no time. Atta boy, Dave!"

The next day, a Sunday, my column was back in the paper. Headline: "Energy hoppers cost us all more." Lead: "Thousands of electricity customers in Texas are dealing with high bills by skipping out on them and signing up with new providers. They are called 'energy hoppers,' and electricity companies don't like to talk about them. Who can blame the companies?"

Everything was back to normal. Almost.

For a couple of weeks, I worked to overcome the jolt of what happened. I put my head down and followed that reader's advice ("Get back to work") But I felt a shakiness, a sense of shame every time I walked into a room. Someone might recognize me, not for my column photo from the paper, but from my creepy mug shot. "It is invariably saddening," F. Scott Fitzgerald wrote in *The Great Gatsby*, "to look through new eyes at things upon which you have expended your own powers of adjustment."

The questions from friends were asked with tenderness and concern: *How is your son? How are you? What's your status at the newspaper?* A few close friends talked to me with a tone that suggested I was ruined. I was OK, I tried to explain. Austin was OK, too. Yet he was not immune from teasing. One group of older boys taunted him at school by chanting, "Your dad left you at McDonald's!"

After years of being battered by people angry at my column, I was better prepared for the criticism than my son, although he handled it remarkably well, considering he read web postings about him at night from anonymous strangers. But I had training in damage control. Knew how to pick myself up after a fall. When you get fired from the Metropolitan Opera before puberty and get reduced to tears by a TV producer at 30 Rockefeller Plaza when you're not old enough to drive, you learn how to roll with the punches. Nevertheless, the McDonald's imbroglio was a huge hit.

I now wore my scarlet letter—"A" for abandonment. As Hawthorne wrote about Hester's predicament, "that scarlet letter, so fantastically embroidered and illuminated ... had the effect of a spell, taking her out of the ordinary relations with humanity, and inclosing her in a sphere by herself."

Two weeks after the charges were dropped that sphere began to open a bit. I remember driving through Watauga (at the speed limit) and starting to relax about it all. Life was returning to normal. Then the cell phone rang. It was the vice president of circulation at my newspaper. He said he was concerned and wanted to know if everything was OK.

"Why?"

"Because my mother is watching Fox News and Megyn Kelly is reporting that you're in trouble again."

I hung up and called my lawyer. He said nothing had happened. I rushed home and turned on Fox News. There was nothing about me. I looked up the network's phone number in New York and worked in vain trying to fool the network's automated viewer comment line into connecting me with a human. Then found a website, not Fox's, listing the network's New York executives by title with direct phone numbers. Left a message for the company's top media-relations man. The executive called back, and I asked what Fox had reported. He said he would look into it and call me back. A few minutes later, he e-mailed me a video of Kelly's segment. I clicked on the link and watched.

Kelly's Court, a feature on Kelly's show "America's Newsroom," places Kelly, a former lawyer, as the "judge" in a dispute between two lawyers with opposing views. Her tagline in Fox News ads reads: "Two sides to every story. One anchor delivers both."

I was topic *du jour*. "Kelly's Court is back in session," she announced. "On the docket today, he left his 11-year-old boy at McDonald's." My mug shot was shown, big enough to fill the screen. Former prosecutor Julia Morrow of Philadelphia was going to put me away. Defense lawyer David Wohl of Los Angeles was going to save me.

The pretend prosecutor started in: "You gotta love the irony of this story. Here's a guy who spends his days at the newspaper fighting big-business bullies. And yet he's a bully himself. Look what he did here.

... He should be facing felony charges."

Judge Kelly weighed in: "Two felony charges? The kid's fine."

My TV lawyer defended me: "That is crazy, Megyn. Was it inappropriate? Yes. Was it boneheaded? Yes. Was it criminal? No. Look, the child was 11 years old, which puts him right about that age that kids can care for themselves for short periods of time. It was a low-crime suburb. It was only a few blocks from his home. And when dad cooled off after a few minutes, he turned right back around and went to pick up Junior."

The prosecutor lunged: "You've got the issue of child predators. I mean, nice middle-class neighborhoods aren't immune to child predators prowling around in their vans looking for lone kids."

My guy responded: "Would I ever leave my son, who's almost 11 years old? No. No. Never."

Thanks for the strong defense, pal.

Then came Judge Kelly's ruling:

"Criminal charges are not appropriate here. This guy made a bad decision, but it didn't result in any harm. This particular case seems like one of a well-meaning law enforcement officer who may have taken things just a bit too far, given the circumstances. Lesson learned for the dad. Let's all move on."

Thank you, judge, for the favorable ruling. But there was one remaining problem. The case was already closed. I called the Fox executive and asked for a correction. He told me to watch the next day's broadcast.

The next day, between stories about President Bush visiting Galveston to view Hurricane Ike damage and discussion about a new poll in the Obama-McCain presidential race, Fox News flashed my mug shot big on the screen. Again.

"A Kelly's Court follow-up for you now," anchor Bill Hemmer said. "Well, the charges against Mr. Lieber were dropped two weeks ago. As was discussed here yesterday, the child was unharmed and Mr. Lieber turned around a short time after he left the restaurant to go back and get his son. All is well there."

All was almost well. I appreciated the correction, but was surprised that Fox didn't do its homework before going live on the air with a stale story that it brought back to life. A simple Google News search would have been enough. Asking obvious questions on stories is a dying art.

Eight months after that, it happened again. This time, though, to somebody else. Madlyn Primoff was a 45-year-old Park Avenue bankruptcy lawyer. She lived with her husband and two daughters in a $2 million home in the affluent New York suburb of Scarsdale. For these reasons of status, occupation and the hungry New York news media, and because she is a mom, rather than a dad, her case attracted great notoriety and debate.

Here's what happened: On a Sunday night, she was driving her daughters, 12 and 10, and their grandmother through suburban White Plains. Her two girls were misbehaving, so Primoff pulled a Dave Lieber and ordered them out of the car. The mother and grandmother drove around the block. The oldest daughter caught up with the mom's car. Primoff let her back in. But they couldn't find the 10-year-old.

A passerby, later described in New York media accounts as "a good Samaritan," found the girl crying on a street corner. He bought her some ice cream at a nearby Carvel store and notified a passing police car. Police drove the 10-year-old to the station. A police report described the child as being upset and emotional.

The mother drove home, told her husband what happened, and then called police to report her missing child. Police told her that her daughter was safe and invited Primoff to come get her. It was a ploy. When Primoff arrived at the station, she was arrested and charged with endangering the welfare of a child. She was kept in jail overnight. A temporary restraining order placed against her meant that, at first, she couldn't be around her children.

The public was split. She was defended; she was vilified. Primoff and her own creepy mug shot of angst and disheveled hair was a contrast to her official law firm portrait. Both images were shared with the world with one memorable headline: "Bankruptcy attorney by day, bad mom on weekends." Her case was featured on the *Today* show, in *The New York Times*, in media outlets across the nation. A producer for ABC's *Good Morning America* called and asked if I would give an interview to help them tell the story. I declined but made sure to watch the show.

The segment began with a scene from ABC's *Desperate Housewives*. Mom Lynette Schiavo tosses her sons out of the car: "I am not going to tell you again. Sit. Out! Can't behave? You heard me. You cannot ride!"

Several parents who practice what the report

called a "you-squawk-you-walk" policy shared their experience. Darlene from Alabama raised six children and said she "routinely" made each of them walk home to teach them there are consequences to their actions. Lesley from Pennsylvania said that she forced her daughter to walk home seven miles in platform shoes. It happened 10 years ago, but she still feels guilty about it.

Science, the report continued, has shown that when people become angry, the part of their brain that handles judgment becomes impaired. Then Ann Pleshette Murphy—known on her website as "America's favorite parenting expert"—offered advice to host Robin Roberts. She said parents should be clear about their expectations to their children. They should set consequences for their actions. If a child must be put out of the car, America's favorite parenting expert said, don't do it "unless you are maybe a block from home and you go with the car alongside them."

"What you said sounds wonderful," Roberts interrupted. "But in the real world, it happens. They implode."

"Yeah, I know," America's favorite parenting expert said. "It does. But really being in touch with how you're feeling is so key. So many mothers hold it in and hold it in and then when we lose it—and I say, we, really, mindfully, because I, of course, have been there—we act in a way that is just not OK."

On ABC's *The View*, Free-Range Kids movement leader Lenore Skenazy returned to the show and defended Primoff, to the dismay of the other women on the panel. She said, "It was a bad parenting moment. I wouldn't do it, but I'm really sorry that the whole country is weighing in on it because we all have bad parenting moments, and we're so judgmental of every parenting decision now from childbirth to breastfeeding to when you let them walk to school."

In court, Primoff's lawyer told a judge that the family had entered therapy. The judge ruled that if there was no more trouble in the family for six months, Primoff's misdemeanor charge would be dismissed.

Outside the courthouse, Primoff apologized in front of TV cameras: "Clearly, I made a mistake. But I truly love our children, and I know I am a good parent."

I wrote a letter to Primoff. We are members of a small club wearing the scarlet letter A. She didn't reply.

Every day, I look at Austin and cheer on his attempts to control his Lieber belligerent gene. Every day, I cheer myself on to do the same.

If I listened to many of the Internet posters, I would have smacked some sense into him, forced him to toe the line, showed him who's boss, ordered him to fetch a branch from the backyard, read him the riot act, benched him from sports, games, television, computer and everything else he loves about life and then, for good measure, sent him to bed hungry. Those were actual suggestions.

If I had to offer two methods that do work, they are these: kindness and patience.

Everybody sees things differently, and every family is different. What works for one family might not work

My three kids: Desiree, Austin and Jonathan.

for another. When I met Desiree, she was 11, and Jonathan was 9. Becoming their stepdad was a terrific honor and responsibility. They welcomed me. Desiree and Jonathan craved a father. From them, I received my parental training.

They, of course, had their own strains of the belligerent gene, from their father. The gene can be found in most families to some degree, whether it's acknowledged or not. Even "America's favorite parenting expert" admits haltingly on national TV that she, too, has the same problem: *"... and then when we lose it—and I say, we, really, mindfully, because I, of course, have been there."*

You can't smack a kid, as so many Internet posters suggested, or decline to feed him, press his nose against the Green Wall or even send him on a 14-minute walk home and expect things to get better.

Carl Honoré, author of *Under Pressure: Rescuing Our Children From the Culture of Hyper-Parenting*, once told *Time*: "People feel there's somehow a secret formula for parenting, and if we just read enough books and spend enough money and drive ourselves hard enough, we'll find it, and all will be OK. Can you think of anything more sinister, since every child is so different, every family is different? Parents need to block out the sound and fury from the media and other parents. Find that formula that fits your family best."

I have read parenting books and talked to experts. In my case, I learned to control those impulses that led to trouble, channeling them into a related career (a dominant belligerent gene may be a necessity for a newspaper columnist). Getting older, slower, calmer, wiser, that helps a lot, too. Then there are those rare hellish days, like that day at McDonald's, when I fall off the wagon and land in the town of Belligerentville all over again.

What did I learn from this? Aside from understanding that I must never lose focus on my father-son love, attention and duty, I know that—no matter my relationship with that particular police department—I must not blame anyone else for placing myself in that vulnerable situation. One of my heroes is Epictetus, a Greek philosopher who spoke about the need for people to take responsibility for their own lives and circumstances. He said, "To accuse others for one's own misfortunes is a sign of want of education. To accuse oneself shows that one's education has begun. To accuse neither oneself nor others shows that one's education is complete."

Thanks to this episode, I have my own formula that fits my family best. This technique helps remind me to do the right thing even when that part of my brain that handles judgment overheats. When the belligerent gene kicks in, I tell myself that I'm on camera, being recorded for anyone and everyone to see. I'm always on camera. If it's not a security camera overhead, then someone has a cell phone camera. Even if they don't, I pretend they do. That's like counting to 10. It works for me.

Each year more of our public spaces are monitored by surveillance cameras seeking intruders, shoplifters, criminals and terrorists. But they also capture everything else. The mother who spanks her child as they exit a Wal-Mart. The teenage driver who weaves in and out of traffic. The drunk trying to buy cigarettes at the 7-Eleven. The leap from staggering alone in a parking lot one day to being shown on Fox News as topic *du jour* the next day is one that anybody ... anybody ... can make these days.

Disneyland was one of the first mainstream American locales that placed itself under complete camera coverage. Casinos followed, then banks, airports, retail stores and schools. Now, as costs have dropped and federal dollars for homeland security have funded their proliferation across the land, cameras are on streetlights, in corridors, and in your pocket on a cell phone.

Imagining that I am always on camera helps me keep my dignity and behave properly. It's a way to rein in any impulses to yell, curse, hit, slap, spank, denounce, belittle, moralize and anything else that might happen when your kids do what kids do—push your buttons and drive you crazy.

So that's my 11th Commandment: *Live your life as if you're always on camera.* Don't do anything you don't want seen by millions.

It shouldn't be hard to do. We ought to be proud to be parents, proud to be good parents, and know always that the titles of Proud Parent and Successful Parent do not come without work. There is no more important job. And I know that what I did that day at McDonald's was beneath the dignity of any dad. I told my son to walk home to make a point, teach him a lesson, help him become a better person, not to place him in danger. It failed, and for a few weeks, our world turned upside down.

Now, thanks to my 11th Commandment, I work to keep the belligerent gene in check. Austin does the same in his own way.

And I watch my speed and count my blessings every day I drive down that strip of roadway in the neighboring city of Watauga.

THE AFTERMATH

Watauga Police Chief Rande Benjamin was removed from office in 2010 by a unanimous vote of the City Council. Twenty-nine officers from the rank of sergeant down had signed a no-confidence complaint. Among the objections: Benjamin ordered a hidden microphone installed in the patrol room to monitor conversations, and he allowed "his personal feelings and animosities to influence his decisions to initiate internal affairs investigations and to proclaim harsh punishments." He was demoted to lieutenant.

Bill Crawford, who had switched from the police department to the fire department, was promoted in 2007 to Watauga fire chief.

Bill Keating, the former city manager and police chief who became a sheriff in 2004, lost re-election in 2008. As he was leaving office, federal and state prosecutors charged him with crimes related to his forcing female inmates to have sex with him and other abuses in his jail. In 2009, he pleaded guilty to a federal civil-rights violation. He died of a heart attack before his sentencing.

Longtime Tarrant County District Attorney Tim Curry passed away in 2009 after serving 36 years. Since then, prosecutors in the district attorney's office have followed up on various Watchdog columns and won criminal convictions.

The city of Watauga attracted attention in 2010 when police arrested a campaign volunteer for holding a political sign on public property. It was Election Day, and the volunteer was standing far enough from the polls, yet police ordered him to get rid of the sign. When he refused, he was jailed. The city later dropped charges and changed its ordinance so people can carry signs on public property. The Liberty Institute, which seeks to protect constitutional freedoms, filed a federal lawsuit against the city on the man's behalf. The lawsuit claims that when the man was jailed on Election Day, he lost his right to participate in the election process.

Texas Gov. Rick Perry vetoed a bill passed by the Texas Legislature in 2009 that would have allowed the expunction of criminal records 180 days after an arrest, if no formal misdemeanor or felony charges have been filed.

Lenore Skenazy continues to serve as the Generalissimo of the Free-Range Kids movement. In 2010, she organized the first "Take Our Children to the Park & Leave Them There Day" as a way to teach children how to play by themselves without constant supervision. You can follow her work on her website (freerangekids.com) and on Twitter @ FreeRangeKids.

And Austin Lieber and his father continue to work (and play) at having the best father-son relationship they possibly can.

BAD DAD Online

 www.BadDadBook.com
(conversations, blog, videos, pictures, updates and more)

 www.facebook.com/BadDadBook

 @DaveLieber, use hashtag #BadDadBook

 www.BadDadBook.com/blog

 www.YouTube.com/BadDadBook

DaveLieber Dave Lieber
So what do y'all think of my story? Have you had
similar experiences as either a parent or a child?
#BadDadBook

Momservations Kelli Wheeler
After reading #BadDadBook, I will definitely shut my
windows the next time I yell at my children. Welcome
to the era of over-your-shoulder parenting.
#BadDadBook.

FreeRangeKids Lenore Skenazy
Why does old-fashioned childhood sound so radi-
cal? Kids deserve freedom we had. It's good for them!
#BadDadBook.

magpie99 Maggie Van Ostrand
Misadventures of Huckleberry Lieber and his
difficult, determined dad teach us it's not our father's
discipline anymore. #BadDadBook

lieber011 Austin Lieber
Dad, a #BadDadBook about us? OK, yeah. But now on
Twitter? Dad? Really?

Join the conversation by adding
#BadDadBook to your tweets.

ABOUT DAVE LIEBER

Dave Lieber, a newspaperman for more than 30 years, never won a Pulitzer Prize, but the first time he rode a bull in Texas, he stayed on for 10 seconds.

 Eight seconds where the bull just stood there, and another 1.6 seconds out in the arena before Dave fell off. Dave rounded that 9.6 seconds up to 10 seconds and felt proud. But actually, Dave was flying through the air longer than he was on that bull.

Dave falls a lot. As this book details, Dave got fired as a gingerbread boy, a singing part he played as a youngster in *Hansel and Gretel* at the Metropolitan Opera. He also got in a heap of trouble when he worked as a 14-year-old hosting a national TV show live on NBC. And then there's the time he was emcee and fell off a stage into the orchestra pit at a high school talent show. That made *America's Funniest Home Videos*.

But Dave doesn't always fall.

As a longtime columnist for the *Fort Worth Star-Telegram*, Dave helps people through his investigations and stories. He's the founder of Watchdog Nation (WatchdogNation.com), which shows Americans how to fight back and win in battles against crooks, scammers and corporate thugs. His book, *Dave Lieber's Watchdog Nation: Bite Back When*

Businesses and Scammers Do You Wrong, won two national book awards for social change.

He's co-founder of Summer Santa Inc., one of North Texas' largest children's charities. An all-volunteer charity, SummerSanta.org helps thousands of at-risk and abused children each year with summer camp scholarships, free medical checkups, back-to-school clothing, school supplies, after-school activities and summertime toys.

For this, Dave won the Will Rogers Humanitarian Award, which goes each year to the newspaper columnist "whose work best exemplifies the high ideals of the beloved philosopher-humorist who used his public forum for the benefit of his fellow human beings."

Dave is also one of Texas' most sought-after speakers. He inspires audiences and teaches them the latest information through humor and storytelling.

Learn more about Dave, his books and his public speaking at YankeeCowboy.com, DaveLieber.org and WatchdogNation.com. Visit his store at YankeeCowboy.com/store.

ACKNOWLEDGMENTS

Special thanks to the *Fort Worth Star-Telegram*, the best newspaper Dave ever worked for, especially Executive Editor Jim Witt and Managing Editor/News and Investigations Lois Norder. For nearly 20 years, both have offered unwavering support, wisdom and expertise in shaping Dave into a journalist whose primary mission is to help people.

Much love to Karen Lieber, Dave's soul mate, and their three children, Desiree, Jonathan and, of course, Austin, to whom this book is dedicated.

Thanks to these news organizations for the privilege of reprinting a portion of their material: *Fort Worth Star-Telegram*; "FrontBurner," the blog of Dallas' city magazine, *D Magazine*; *Fort Worth Weekly*; Fox News; *Wall Street Journal*; *Austin American-Statesman*; and *Philadelphia* magazine.

Finally, thanks to book designer Janet Long; book editor Art Carey; copy editors Anita Robeson and Stan Lieber; cover expert Norm Sunshine (SunshineProductionsOnline.com); speech coach Doug Stevenson (Storytelling-in-Business.com); web gurus Stuart Perry and Jon Perry (RebelWithoutApplause.com) and Thomas Umstattd Jr. (AuthorTechTips.com); credit card partner Vanessa Lang (MerchantServices.cc); marketing aces Ed Peters and Homer Plankton; sounding boards Wil Haygood, Kelly Bradley, Jim Maine, Randy Pugh, Mike Blackman and Jennifer Hall; lawyer Tim Moore; and last, but dare not least, Austin's grandmother and Dave's mother-in-law,

Joan Pasciutti, who gets a special shout-out for putting up with it all. Can't be easy.

DAVE LIEBER is a popular international speaker with a rare gift: he combines a lifetime of observation with the ability to hold audiences spellbound through the use of comedy and emotional storytelling techniques.

He will craft a memorable message to help your group achieve its goals. To learn more, call or look online.

1-800-557-8166
E-mail: Speaker@YankeeCowboy.com
Websites:
YankeeCowboy.com • DaveLieber.org
WatchdogNation.com